DROPSHIPPING

E-COMMERCE

A Must-read Beginner's Guide to Dropshipping on How to Customize Your Own Brand Store, Find the Best Niche Content Which Will Keep Customers Coming Back!

I0499893

Table of Contents

Introduction

Congratulations on purchasing Dropshipping E-commerce: A Must-read Beginner's Guide to Dropshipping on How to Customize Your Own Brand Store, Find the Best Niche Content Which Will Keep Customers Coming Back! and thank you for doing so. This book is for individuals who are interested in starting a drop shipping online business. It may seem like a very hectic process, but with time and a lot of practice, you'll be successful.

Through this book, you will get all the information that is needed to start and manage a dropshipping business. You will get to know about what dropshipping means, the pros, and cons of this business. There is more information on how you can be successful in the business. You will be informed of the supply business in dropshipping, and it is importance in the business.

This is an online business that involves a lot of ordering and shipment. It is important you know about the best suppliers, the bad ones, how you'll be ordering, and how to choose the best products to list.

With the rise in technology, dropshipping is also not left out. You'll know of the Oberlo app, its advantages, and its disadvantages. Before ordering, you need to know of the right suppliers; you'll get all this information from the suppliers' directory. Finally, yet importantly, the book has illustrated all the pricing strategy that you can use. There is also a glossary to help you understand all the terminologies.

This topic is broad, and there are several books available. Thank you for taking the time and picking this book as your final choice. All the efforts were put in to ensure you get a detailed and useful book. Enjoy your reading.

Chapter 1: What is Dropshipping?

What is Dropshipping?

If you are new to the Dropshipping Business and seeking to venture into the e-commerce arena, this venture can seem overwhelming.

Dropshipping is a retail fulfillment method where the store does not keep the goods itself. Instead, the Customer purchase the product from the retailer, the retailer transfers customer orders to the manufacturer or another retailer to ship the product directly to the customer. The retailer pays the manufacturer and the customer received the order.

The product is not handled by the retailer at all.

It is an extremely attractive business model as the retailer does not have to complete any inventory at the end of their financial year or have a physical business location to store any of his product listed in their website.

The Merchant only needs a laptop and an internet connection.

Dropshipping is not time-consuming, and you don't need much capital to begin with.

In this guide, we will learn the essential knowledge, resource, and you will be equipped with the right tools to be able to set up a successful dropshipping business.

The Advantages of Dropshipping

As a business model, dropshipping has many advantages and disadvantages, and it's relevant to learn and get knowledge before considering starting a dropshipping business. We will go through the advantages and disadvantages of dropshipping, and at the end of this guide, running a dropshipping business effectively will be a breeze!

Some of the advantages that prove to be beneficial are:

- **Launching this business is easy.**

No level of academic qualification or professionalism is required to start. By learning the concepts and how to apply them, you can begin and learn the rest as you go along.

There are fewer requirements needed to begin. Mainly, there are three steps:

- Get the supplier

- Create your website

- Start selling your products.

There is no need to find a warehouse or hiring a team to help you manage the business. It's not time-consuming, as you don't need to spend many hours at the store. It's non-restrictive when the business picks up.

Dropshipping business is easy to implement, especially for a beginner.

- **Less capital required.**

It's very easy to start an e-commerce business as we only pay our products after the customer has paid us upfront. Literally, we can start without investing thousands of dollars in inventory.

Compared to the others traditional business set up, where retailers had to spend a lot of capital on purchasing inventory, the Dropshipping gives the opportunity to anyone to begin an online business with very little capital.

- **Flexibility**

One of the huge benefits of Dropshipping is, you make all the decisions on how to run your business by yourself, and you can set the right work schedule that will be perfect with your day to day activities.

The Dropshipping best suits the person who wants a business that works for them without having a boss telling you what to do every time, and you can get to set your own space. You can take as much time you need to make decisions that are best for your business. New product listing is very important, and you can change and adjust your strategies at any time.

Also, if you are away for some time, you can automate everything to run smoothly. Having an excellent communication between your customers and suppliers, managing your business will be a success.

If you understand this business model, the possibilities are endless.

- **The risks are significantly lower.**

The risk is almost to none in this business. If there are no sales, no loss would incurred, as the product is paid only after the customers have paid us.

- **No enormous overhead costs.**

Since you won't be buying stock and need any storage room, there will be no worries of paying rental bills and utility bills like electrical and phone bill. The Expenses will be very little.

- **Minimized product damage.**

The item is shipped from the supplier straight to the customer. The shipment goes directly from the supplier to the customer; As the retailers doesn't handle the product at all, the shipping process, minimized the damages on the shipped item.

- **Variety of products**

Offering a variety of products in your business is a goal to aim at, it is possible with the dropshipping business. The different sizes of your product and the storage won't be a problem because the items are listed on the website, and the order is handled by the supplier.

The Disadvantages of Dropshipping

The advantages of dropshipping are great, but in life, there must be a positive and a negative side. And this business is also not excluded. Here are some of the disadvantages to the dropship business model:

- **Profit margin is less.**

When you start a business, in the early stages, the profit margin will be a bit lower, but that won't be the case in the long run, it will start to grow. The Niche that you will choose will play a huge role in your profit margin. A very-competitive niche can affect your profit earning.

If you follow this guide, I guaranteed you that you will learn how to choose the most profitable product. This can be improved by picking the perfect niche. In the long run, you will be earning a greater profit margin.

This business model depends on and relies on sales to be profitable. The prices for the dropshipping products will be determined by the merchant's niche, location, and the requirements for each product. If the retailers start their business and set their prices very low, in a very competitive niche, thinking it will help to increase sales, I am sorry to tell you that it will only results in a lower profit margin. I will suggest taking your product off from the website and substitute with a better profitable one!

The good news is, you can avoid all these by choosing a niche that will be the best fit for your business.

- **Order processing can become difficult.**

The order process can look easy, from customer order to the supplier shipping the order. It can be an easy process, but you might run into some problems if you are sourcing multiple products from different suppliers. Shipping different products can be dramatic, and at a higher cost, also different suppliers have different methods for processing, billing, and shipping. A scenario like when a customer orders two different items from two suppliers, you will incur the cost of shipping the items to the customer. You won't be able to charge the customer the extra cost of shipping, as this will affect the final price of the customer when they pay. The price will be higher and can lead to fewer sales, thus less profit margin.

- **Liability when something goes wrong.**

When the supplier makes a mistake with the customer's order, the retailer must take the responsibility, apologize to the customer and contact the supplier to correct the mistake. Also, selling low quality products, sending the wrong packaging, sending damaged and delivering late can destroy your business reputation. Low-quality packing can damage your business image. You can avoid all these problem by getting a great supplier beforehand.

- **Not having product information can be an issue.**

Since the retailer does not store the goods that they sell, they cannot give specific information about the item. The supplier might not have listed the item description. You will not be able to answer customer's questions or concerns about the item description like the weight, dimensions, usage of the item, and so on. You will constantly have to forward the customer's inquiries to the supplier.

Less information leads to providing less useful content on your website, which will also damage your SEO. To avoid all the above, before start selling the product ask the supplier for an example to be sent home with all the product's details.

- **Poor customer support.**

The retailers need to be very careful of how long the supplier takes to deliver the products to the customer. As it is the supplier sending directly the product to the customer, we have no control over them. It is important to track down each delivery on a daily basis, to see where the package is located. The disadvantage is, the retailer will have to take the blame when there is a complaint from the customer.

- **Competition is very high.**

Popularity in this business model means competition from your fellow retailers in every niche. Profits can be low as you are basically selling the exact same thing as tons of other online stores. The solution here is, the retailer must choose a perfect niche, to reduce the competition and follow the hot trendy Niches of the moment!

How to be Successful in the Dropshipping Business

After going through the advantage and the disadvantage of dropshipping, it is relevant to learn and understand the facts well before considering starting this business. The cons can be avoided if there are a clear understanding and planning between the supplier and the retailer. With better planning, these cons can be prevented.

Anyone can start a dropshipping business. But the business to be a success and be ranked high with other great and already developed business, you must work smart and have the knowledge needed to succeed. With low capital needed to begin, you need to have a better plan. Here are some steps to follow to be able to succeed in this business:

- **Niche**

Research and find a unique niche that it's of interest to you. Choose a niche that you are passionate about. As they say, choose a job you love, and you will never work a day in your life. Like any other new business, it will take a lot of hard work to start and sustain a dropshipping business successfully. There are some components to consider before choosing a niche. These are: Irresistible profits, unique products that will appeal to the customer, lower shipping cost, using online marketing tools like Keyword Planner to check search terms which are associated with your niche and rebranding your products can make you stand from your competitors, and it will add more value to your business.

- **Market research**

The competition in this business field is high since low capital is needed to start. A lot of new dropshipping businesses fail due to the wrong choice of product to sell. Product with less to no competition can be the downfall of a dropshipping business. There are many reasons why such a product has no competition. The reason as such, the product can have a high cost in shipping, which can lead to low-profit margins. The best idea is to choose products that have high competition since they have a higher demand and business sustainability.

- **Find the right supplier.**

By not finding the right supplier can have a negative impact on your business. A supplier has an important role in your business. Before choosing a supplier, do your research properly. Most suppliers you find might not be in your location, and some not even in the same country you are. It can be a problem in terms of communication channels or even a language barrier. The solution here is to make sure that there is no hindrance and, if these issues can't be sorted out, then it's better to find another supplier who can meet all your requirements.

- **Build a website.**

Consider getting a website for your business. This is important as the website will represent what you sell. It's your store. The customer will be able to look at the products that you sell, and they can make orders. You don't need to be a computer wizard to create an e-commerce website but Make it Yours!

- **Build a marketing strategy.**

You have chosen the right products, created the perfect website, but all this can be invalid if customers are not looking at your website, and there are no sales. You must have the perfect marketing strategy to increase traffic to your website. One of the ways to increase traffic is through Social Media and sending Emails to previous customers to inform them of new products that you have added on your website. These marketing strategies will give you a boost to your revenue.

- **Analyze and optimize**

By tracking every sale, you will be able to know, every demand for each of your product, the type of customer ordered your item and what the customer wants. The retailer must always be on the lookout for special requirements and trends. Getting potential customers to and increase your sales.

Chapter 2: What is the Supply Chain in Dropshipping?

Supply Chain in Dropshipping

A supply chain is a name developed in the service industry to describe the path that a product at any given time takes from conception, which is at the production stage, to the hands of its designated consumer in a market. This supply chain can, at times, include the conception stages at which it is mined, refined and prepared.

Three parties are always required to maintain the supply chain:

- **Manufacturers**

At this stage, they are responsible for the creation of the product and in almost all cases, they don't sell the product directly to the public but prefer a strategy of selling as batches to retailers and wholesalers.

The production and running costs at this level are at their minimal for each product, thus provide a positive stride environment for resales. The main reason why it is hard to purchase from this stage is due to economies of scale raised by packing, transporting, and repacking goods for each consumer at this level.

The manufacturers will almost always be geographically present close to their resources than their markets. This usually makes it hard for consumers to access their stores while making it hard for manufacturers to manage any stores set up away from them but closer to consumers.

- **Wholesalers**

They order products in bulk from the manufacturer, most often tweak them a little bit, then place a price and sell them to the public. At times they can end up selling products at a lower cost compared to that set by a manufacturer due to factors that influence market prices.

Wholesalers usually tend to operate in their preferred industry, providing slight variations in product options. They tend to restrain their sale books to retailers rather than interacting directly with consumers.

- **Retailers**

These are a group of people in a business market that are responsible for selling products directly to the consumer or anyone at the end of the product chain. Thus, anyone who runs their customer orders via drop shipping will be termed as a retailer.

This fact will thus mean since a wholesaler or a manufacturer can decide to engage in dropshipping, he/ she will not act as a retailer since drop shipping is now a service. Without the dynamics of the supply chain, most consumers would end up having to buy their products from the manufacturer.

This would create a chaotic market as most complimentary products are produced at different locations, meaning a consumer would travel distances for even the smallest of products. The supply chain involves the production and logistics necessary to keep a consumer most satisfied, which in turn leads to more consumption. This, in any market, is one of the core factors for a business to thrive.

A reliable supply chain has two driving mechanisms. These are namely efficiency and reliability. The efficiency deals with the optimization of all energy placed to deliver the required qualities that a consumer looks up to at a minimum cost while reliability tries to ensure the standards of the product are maintained throughout the supply chain. These mechanisms are usually driven up or down depending on a market demand, which is by default under the consumers, together as one, control. A well-planned supply chain will thus play a crucial affordability task in every product under the line.

In most cases, there is a lot of discussions that go on where consumers try to maximize on their desired features against those offered by every product. This explains why a satisfied consumer today might buy a modified product tomorrow.

Marketing every product in the market may, at times, shift the opinion of the consumer since the consumer is more limited to the practicality of a product in his/her environment.

With internet swamping the producer-consumer connectivity, dropshipping has reinvented itself while getting rid of traditional methods.

Dropshipping has allowed producers and consumers to avoid the hectic work of inventory and delivery, leaving room for better product strategies. This has allowed manufacturers to prevent the risks associated with logistics while reducing the enormous variations developed by consumers individually ordering a product from the manufacturer. Dropshipping has also allowed the manufacturer to coordinate with almost perfect tuning to the demands of the markets. This means that in case one product is instantly at a higher demand than the other, the manufacturer will almost immediately become aware due to the nature of the orders arriving. This allows the manufacturer to protect itself from the market over-saturation of a product, which can cause the market value to drop down, leading to losses. This will also directly cause the superior product that by now is running low on the stock to drive its prices higher. This, in a more prolonged effect, can affect product brands among the consumer markets.

The fact that drop shipping allows orders to be run close to the market and further from the manufacturer means that the manufacturer knows from who to obtain consumer input. Consultation on products by the manufacturer, becomes more natural and effective as data can be collected and analyzed in real-time via the primary tool in use, the internet.

A major problem developed in this type of supply chain is that the drop shipper neither handles the product in the sale nor it takes to deliver to the consumer. The customer satisfaction is out of the retailer control and it means that the drop-shipper is less proactive in the sale and exposure of the product. Fortunately, since technology is involved, the drop-shipper can maximize consumer experience during the deal while the wholesalers or the manufacturer maximize the efficiency and product quality.

This method of a supply chain will always benefit the wholesalers as serving multiple retailers will reduce the cost of holding inventory, marketing, and customer handling. Over time, the good relations between the drop shipper and retailers begin to pay off via a fully functioning system or response and surveys, making it an effective method.

The Importance of Supply Chain in Dropshipping

Due to drop shipping getting rid of the need for physical warehouses, the need for inventory at every level is reduced. The manufacturer can move his product from his production line directly to the supplier or retailer. The retailer also reduces the number of suppliers he/she will need to keep a good contact to increase profits and efficient delivery. The drop shipper in this supply chain will act with efficiency to deliver the product when most required by the consumer from the producer.

Due to the supplier being actively involved with orders from the producer, there is a reduction of stock-outs, thus will most satisfy a customer as he/ she will be able to obtain products at his/ her convenience. This method of supply chain usually allows the retailer and supplier to track orders in real-time, bringing about a transparent logistics method for both parties. Through this method, more trust is developed among members of the same market; thus, satisfaction levels can be transferred across the platform with the product gaining the most advantage.

Due to the accuracy of product consumption available to both the retailer and producer, the forecast activity can be carried out with minimal error variations, thus can help analyze performances at different seasons, monitor real-time activity, and plan promotional trips depending on the available opportunities. While the supplier does a forecast, the retailer can use these market charts, thus reducing the cost of having to carry out the analyses.

The dropship model has been noticed to help reduce the margins between the apex and crest periods of consumptions during production, which will then allow satisfaction based on quality and delivery at the consumers' end throughout the season. This helps develop a trusted and reliable brand. This has been noted to cause brands to gain popularity even across other lines of products.

Dropshipping method due to his real-time, orders can effectively cause logistics to be way cheaper compared to point delivery where production line always takes one end. Through this system, the supplier runs the resupply process allowing them to maintain the broader brand market scope over their market. Customers at all points will be able to choose locations at which they can obtain their products, unlike where they must be in specific retailer shops to decide what is offered hoping it suits their demand features.

Manufacturers will tend to be the first to benefit from this chain as they get to negotiation tables first by negotiating for more exceptional margins. The retailers, at times, end up missing from the chain, as discussed earlier. The manufacturer can also sell expensive and exquisite products through more retailers, thus increasing the range of high-end price list with no storage risks involved. Dropshipping will, along the entire chain, lower the labor and space required to sell each product to the market.

This method of marketing will also allow retailers to sell a wide range of products, which is basically limited by the size of items they can temporarily hold. At times inventory is only established to verify to a consignment of a product to the consumer during delivery. The popularity of marketing space accounted for e-commerce makes it hard for manufacturers to shy away from their consumers. This type of exposure has helped drop shipping develop exponentially over time. Dropshipping allows for speedy consumption of products in the market, thus increase in profitability per commodity. With a well-managed environment, it is possible to maintain satisfaction levels at a high note encouraging even more consumers to participate in the brand. This is a common trend towards commodities such as clothes.

Dropshipping has allowed manufacturers to reach a much wider geographical market such as transpacific trading routes by taking advantage of logistical methods that have been developed over the years to accommodate these challenges best.

Dropshipping makes it easy to start compared to other models as one needs an operational website with just items available for sale compared to others where one needs space and capital to reach consumers. Dropshipping also makes it easy to scale up and down whenever required, mostly at a click of a button. It is possible to maintain a tight leash over the products being sold over the platform, the location, and the age of buyers. With the latest region restrictions, dropshipping has made the adaptation to a region much easier and relatable. By use of online tools, one is to bring the language barrier with clients as translation is provided for free. This has made possible to trade between Asia and other English-speaking countries easier and efficient by maintaining the quality of message and expression.

This method has allowed startups to maintain low and healthy cash flow from entrepreneurs as one does not need to spend so much before they start getting their value returns. One does not need to launch a separate website as some of the already established websites such as Amazon allow for the third party to post products for a fraction of the total profit fee. This method will also never result in a bad-buy situation; thus, one would not expect an overstock issue to arise during the projected trade progress.

The biggest advantage that drop shipping has over older models is that it allows retailers and/or consumers to make orders at their place of comfort. This allows for unlimited buy time. It's almost equal to a store that opens twenty-four hours a day to cater for customers who shop at different times only this time around. This has allowed manufacturing industries to work on an optimization schedule on their workstations round the year. This has also reduced the congestion in towns while allowing only physically available stores to run at simplified flexibility to their design.

Dropshipping has had most of its success credited to the wide of the internet, but like all business models, capitalizing on opportunity is what makes the business stand out in the crowd.

Online dropshippers essentially work with technology and customer service, which are crucial aspects in dropshipping. Consider these two basic facts:

1. The wholesaler handles products and logistics.
2. The dropshipper handles sales and customers.

While manufacturers and wholesalers take on the capital- and labor-intensive aspects of consumer market, dropshippers and retailers they consider the most important aspect of retailing: providing a seamless and positive customer experience.

Chapter 3: The Order Process in Dropshipping

When you choose to dropship as your fulfillment option, you need to know that it requires three options: the product list, the inventory, and the orders. The seller and the retailer have something in common, which is the data. This is something that the retailer will not find as tangible. The product listing is a collection of what the product entails. The brand name, the product title, the category used, the images, and any descriptive features. This is, in short, a brief description of the products. Even though it is a description, it should be informative enough to help customers in the purchase decision.

You should use the inventory as a form of data, that will help to know which items you need to buy and where the item is. You will know the quantities and how much the product will cost. The order is what the customer requests in terms of a product. The retailer was selling the product online. The purchase information needs to be sent to the supplier. This is because the supplier has the products, and they will need to ship to the customer.

The ordering process is considered to be two way. There is always the exchange of data and information between the supplier and the retailer. When the supplier gives their information, it is in the form of the inventory and the product list. The orders are from the retailer for the consumption purposes of the supplier. And the fulfillment process is again from the supplier to the retailer. This is done to know if the product needs to be shipped or be canceled.

As compared to the traditional ordering process, dropshipping involves separate order channels. The first one is between the customer and the retailer. There is a virtual or physical point of sale involved and is commonly known as the consumer order. The second one is between the retailer and the suppliers or vendors, and it is known as the purchase order. For the typical supply chain, the purchase order is what comes first; the retailer will buy from the wholesaler. The ordering will then come later when the retailer sells to the consumer.

As for dropshipping, the process is in reverse. The retailer will generate an order from the customer, and then sent the order to the supplier. This will turn to a purchase order from the retailer to the supplier. This is complicated because it involves a lot of back-office procedures, a point of sale, complicated systems, and technologies, but when you get to understand the process and procedures of dropshipping clearly, you will not have a hard time processing all that, and your customers will enjoy the services.

When you decide to automate the whole process, there are some aspects that you will have to know. You need to know how to handle multiple orders. This will normally occur when the suppliers get an order and can only deliver just part of the order. In case you have any backlog or backorders, you need to be able to manage them effectively. The difference with the manual ordering is that, all that is ordered as they come up.

There are challenges expected when you are dealing with orders between retailers, suppliers, and customers. If you have handled all that, including inventory and product listing, then you'll have an easy time engaging with dropshipping. Another contributing factor to having success in dropshipping is when there is a good relationship between the suppliers and retailers and between the demand and supply.

How to Find a Good Supplier

If you want to survive in the dropshipping business, you'll need to get a reliable supplier. You need to be very careful about how you choose one and remember to get one for the long haul. When you get a good supplier, you are entitled to have a stable and constant supply, which will directly help your business. When you fall prey to a bad supplier, you'll jeopardize your business credibility and your hard work. You should know, that getting a good and reliable supplier can be a daunting task.

This chapter will highlight more on how to get a good supplier and additional information. The first thing you need to know is when you suppose to start looking for a supplier; when you are looking for a supplier and a product and when you have already decided of the product you want and you need a supplier. There are several others factors you need to consider when looking for a supplier.

Look for a professional: Always look for a professional. Dropshipping is a professional business, so when you start out, look for professionals. Make sure all the relationships you establish for your business are on a professional level. There are different agreements that need to be drawn to ensure everyone sticks to the regulations. You need to look for reliable and credible suppliers so as not to affect your business.

A punctual supplier: When you pick a professional supplier, you'll be assured of a punctual supplier, a supplier who will not have an issue in time keeping and delivering on time. This is an important factor since it will come handy in terms of shipping. It is important for the shipping procedure to be known, and the deadline met.

Proximity: Even though this factor is not considered a must, it is important to consider it. When you are looking for business ideas, ensure you choose something that is close. When you have suppliers who are close by, it is easier to know them in person.

In case you have any issues with the items delivered or there are delays, you can track them.

Competitors: You need to look for a supplier that is different from your competitors. It will tend to be difficult to operate when customers are not able to differentiate your products from your competitors. You'll have issues to position your brand.

Always ask for a contract: Look for a supplier that will ask for a contract, and that will be coupled with some rules and regulations. You should also ask for a written and signed contract. Ensure the contract has components like communication, what are the communication channels you plan to use when there is an order, how long it will take to deliver the product to the customer. Discuss commission—what is the percentage in the commission that will be given, the payment terms, the method of payment and which is the procedure for the returns and the refunds. The drop shipper can always give out invoices and extend a discount. You should also remember to include any shipping details of what you are selling. Both parties should comply with the stated conditions and regulations. Any compensation details should also be included. You should know that signing a contract is very important. Since you have a professional relationship, it will guide both parties on the rules and regulations to follow. This will be a binding document that will also help in enhancing a good and long-term relationship.

It may be difficult to get a supplier who will meet all the requirements, be patient, and take the time to choose one. There are many out there.

When negotiating with a supplier, ensure you always pay attention and know two important factors. That you have a physical shop and that you are starting from somewhere. There are several practices that you can apply that could help with such negotiating.

- **Do your research.**

The first step in dropshipping is to research what you want. You will start your research after you know about the products that you would like to sell. And research on the suppliers that you desire. Depending on your product category, you'll decide if you would like to go for a local or international supplier. Looking for a supplier involves several options, the availability of raw material, the times they deliver, and the services offered.

- **Contact the suppliers.**

This will help in building a relationship with them. You'll ask questions about the products and services that they offer. They can offer you contact details of their current customers so that you can test and check on their reviews. You will be able to gain their trust in the long run, which will be beneficial to your business.

- **Get samples for the supplier.**

When you've made your mind on the suppliers that you want. Ask them for samples. This will give you the chance to know their quality, their packaging, the delivery time, and any other related questions. When you order samples from them, this will help you to understand and know more about their services, and most importantly, how they will deal with your customers.

- **Always negotiate from a position of power.**

You will be able to get better favors when you operate from a position of power, and it will give you many privileges. You have an added advantage because you are not starting from a position with zero power. The reason will be that you already in a working position, and you have ready and potential buyers. A good example will be like a company that sells bags but had started out as a company that does reviews.

- **Start with no website.**

The only setback with this option is that you do not have anything to show. When you are negotiating, you do not have anything to showcase. Even when you promise several sales, you will not have anything to show. The drop shipper will only trust your word when doing online business. It is sometimes hard to make your drop shipper trust you.

When you do not have enough traffic to your website, it will be hard to negotiate on commission. Dropshipping is not an easy business, and it will need dedication and focus in order to be successful.

- **Make everything legal.**

Ensure that your business is legal before you even carry out and do any business. Suppliers will be adamant about selling their products to you when they know that the business does not have legal papers. And when you get a supplier who is ready to work with you, do not be in a rush. Not all the available suppliers are the best; make an informed decision.

- **Make use of a directory.**

Make sure you look for directories that have suppliers' details from different companies worldwide. You'll be charged a small fee to access their data. These directories will save you a lot of time, and you'll get reliable information. Some of the directories include Salehoo and WholesaleCentral. You need to be informed before you contact them, know about the company, their reviews, and their websites.

- **Make use of Google.**

When you do not get your desired suppliers on the directories, try and use Google. You can search for the items that you want to sell and do an analysis. Since there will be many suppliers, you need to do a thorough search to get your ideal supplier.

- **Know your competitor.**

You should ensure that you know your competitors well, know their products, their prices, and the product sources. A trick you can use is ordering something from them and then returning it when you receive it. You'll be given details about the wholesaler, their names and address.

- **Change of supplier.**

When you get a supplier, who does not meet your needs, it is acceptable to change them. If you do not, it will negatively affect your business. With drop shipping, you should not allow issues with shipping or availability of products. When the order is placed, ensure that everything in that order is sent the same day. Always make a comparison of the products offered and what the competitor is offering, always be on the lookout for new suppliers. If you do not match with your competitor or you are having delivery delays, it will definitely affect your business.

How to Know the Bad Suppliers

When you start doing your research, you'll come across suppliers who are not good—commonly termed as being fake. The main reason for finding the fake ones is because the reliable and good supplies are not into marketing. It is even more difficult to trace them. When doing your searches, ensure that you are very careful of the middlemen. A lot of your searches will bring up more of them. Luckily there are several ways that will help in differentiating a good supplier from a bad one.

Ongoing Fees: Real and genuine suppliers will not ask for fees on a monthly basis to cover for the ordering services and from ordering from them. In case you get one asking for membership fees, that cannot be legitimate. You also need to know the difference between the directories. Supplier directories provide suppliers details based on product categories, and they charge a fee for that. Their charges are either one-off or ongoing, so do not confuse that with the illegal suppliers.

Public Sale: A genuine supplier is a supplier that has a wholesale account. Before getting that genuine account, your documents will be verified and will be legitimate. All this is normally done before placing any order. So, when you get a supplier selling to the public at wholesale prices, you should be careful because that can just be a retailer selling at prices that are inflated. You should also bear in mind some of the fees that are applicable, and they are legitimate.

Preorder Fees: They are charged below $5. The price will depend on the size of the product and how complicated they are. The price is always standard but might tend to be higher as compared to doing a bulk order. You should do your research to ensure that you know of the genuine and not genuine suppliers, especially the ones charging higher than the normal cost. That can be a bad sign and an indication to stay away from such suppliers.

There are other points to watch out for bad suppliers, look for the ones with reviews that are not good, and any feedback that is negative. Most of them will offer products that are cheap and poor quality. These are some of the qualities that can indicate you are dealing with a bad supplier.

Minimum Order Quantity: This is what is commonly known as MOQ. These are the minimum order you can make on any product. It is the lowest quantity for the initial order. The main reason for this is to cut out any suppliers that are not serious. They will waste time asking questions. And most of the time, it will not translate to any sale. It is considered a loss to the business. This is a challenge when you are dropshipping when you're required to do a MOQ of $400, and your required order is $200. This could be a challenge since you'll not be able to order on such conditions that are required just to have an account with the supplier. Most of the suppliers will always charge a fee for the minimum order and for fulfillment. So, when you encounter a supplier who does not want to stick to any minimum order quantity, consider them as wholesalers in dropshipping.

How to Order

A retailer who is into dropshipping can decide on their own way of displaying their products. They can have a physical shop or do it online. When they go the online way, they should ensure that they provide a product listing. This will help the customers have a glimpse of what is being sold and will also help the customers with the purchase decision.

The retailer has the option not to disclose its wholesaler. This can be done by practicing what is known as blind shipping. This is simply referred to as shipping the order without indicating an address that can be used for any returns.

Another option is private label shipping. This happens when an order is placed and shipped from the wholesaler. It will have an address personalized to go back to the retailer. The retailer will then decide to ship the products to their customers directly from the manufacturer. Dropshipping is mostly done for costly products.

At this point, you've clearly understood all that is needed to make an order. You need to know the all whole process of ordering and all the items ordered are shipped from the wholesalers.

- The customer places an order online with the retailer. The order needs to be approved first. The customer will then get a confirmation via email for the order. After going through the checkout process, customers' payment details are captured. The funds will be sent directly to the retailer.

- The wholesaler will now place an order with the supplier. An email will be forwarded to confirm the order from the wholesaler. They will confirm with their sales representative. They will start the billing process and even include all the charges applicable. Some drop shippers use an advanced option of inventory management. This is simply the option to place an order online on a manual basis. The common option still remains to be using email since it is easy to use.

- The items are shipped from the wholesaler's store. This will only happen when the item is considered to be in stock, and the billing went through successfully. That is when the wholesaler will package the items and ship them to the customer. Even though the products are from the wholesaler, the shipping address will be for the supplier.

- It will include the supplier's name, their address as the return address. On the invoice and the slip used for packaging, you'll find the retailer's business logo. When the shipment is completed, the wholesaler will then send an email to the retailer with the invoice and a number that is used for tracking. The advantage of using this type of retailer is that you are guaranteed same-day delivery.

- The retailer will then inform the customer of the items shipped. When they receive the tracking number, the retailer will then send all the tracking information to the customer. This is done via email, and when the order is sent, payment is received, and notification is done. At this point, you can consider that the process of ordering and fulfilling is done. The retailer will then compute their loss or profit based on what they charged the customer and what they paid the wholesaler.

How to Choose the Best Products

There are several ways that you can use to pick the best product for dropshipping. When starting out with the dropshipping business, make sure you are careful about how you choose your products. Do not be in a hurry to pick the products. Ensure you strategically and competitively pick your product categories. There are different ways of selecting products.

- You should consider all the options; your products are the main support for your online business. And the better the product choice, the better your business will be. So, since you've known how important it is when it comes to product selection, be careful. Spare your maximum time doing your research and look for products that are competitive. Look for better products that you would like to offer. Consider the best product categories that are more friendly to e-commerce and create a competitive niche for your business.

- Look for better ideas and fast-moving products. Ensure to look for items that are selling at that time. Look for what the other sellers are offering and how they brand their market station. Look at what the other suppliers are offering and learn from them. Create your own unique and attractive products. Researching will enable you to see an idea and personalize it. You'll be able to see a concept and develop it or better develop it into something better. If you have not made up your mind on what products you want, you can look for the products with higher selling rates.

- You can also start with the products that you have in mind. Like from your hobbies, you like, and also your passion. There are tools that you can use to brainstorm and get product ideas. This includes Google Trends. You can start by looking for information around, and then it will give you a point to start from. Think of all the products that come into your mind and write them down. This is an important step since it will provide more information for the other steps.

- You can also get your ideas from checking information from your competitor's shop. You'll be able to know of the approaches that your competitors are using, and this will help in being competitive. You can start by looking at the way they display, their product list, and if they have any promotions. Research constantly, and you'll get more information. This information is very important when it comes to product selection.

- You can get more information on the products to choose from products that are listed on social sites that allow their customers to shop. You'll have access to a variety of products. The products are available in different categories and trending products. Do not overlook these sites since they are known to offer more information on what you can choose from. It is advisable to sign up for an account with them and have a subscription on different product types and lists. Look at what they prefer the most and what they will choose to buy. When you properly research and look for more information, you'll be able to make a decision on what to sell. And you will be assured of more sales and higher profit margins.

- It is also a good idea to ask ideas from people who are close to you. When you meet your friends or family members, always remember to ask them for their opinions on the products that can sell. Do not limit yourself to what you think will sell. Ask around for different ideas and opinions. You'll be surprised by the information you can get from the external information.

- Look around for any information that will help in making the decision. These places can be at your business place, workplace, and even around your community.

Chapter 4: What is the Oberlo App?

What is the Oberlo App?

Ever had the idea of doing dropshipping with no clue of how to get started? Oberlo application is there for you. Oberlo app is an original dropshipping application popularly for the e-commerce marketplace platform Shopify. This app was founded by a group of close friends in 2015. This application enables users to import items directly from Aliexpress, which is one of the popular online Chinese marketplaces. Oberlo tremendously became popular due to its powerful features and high optimization.

This application cannot be used on a stand-alone website but rather on a Shopify store. Within a short period of time, a drop shipper can import products of preference to a Shopify store using this application and sell them directly to the customer. This app has nearly 7,000 active Shopify stores, which have been able to make 36 million sales.

How Does Oberlo Make Money?

Every time an order is made, some coupons are normally paid out to Oberlo by the Aliexpress sellers. The app also makes money through paid plans, which include a basic plan and a professional plan. The starter plan is free of charge, and you are able to sell up to 500 products and receive 50 orders every month. The basic plan for the Oberlo application monthly cost is

$29.90 purposed mostly for user accounts, which process 500 orders every month. The plan constitutes the shipment tracking and order features. Then there is the professional plan with a monthly cost of $79.90 inclusive of the shipment tracking, order features plus multiple user accounts unlike as it is seen with the basic plan. The plan to be mostly preferred normally depends on the size of your business.

Features of the Oberlo App

Now let's dig deeper into the features of this dropshipping application:

- **Multiple user account feature**

  Oberlo has only one plan, a professional plan, which has this feature of multiple user accounts. This feature is so useful that it enables the entire team to access the application to facilitate the smooth running of the online store.

- **Efficient track of the sales**

  Sales are able to be tracked automatically and monitored. The success of the store is measured at a glance by viewing the most selling product.

- **Automatic track of orders**

Oberlo application is able to track the orders made by the customers automatically. Customers are provided with expected delivery dates and the up to date delivery information.

- **Quick access to Aliexpress products**

  Using this application enables you to add products easily by browsing the big database of Aliexpress. ePacket can also be implemented, which helps you to import products with the quickest time of delivery.

- **Change of product's supplier**

  Aliexpress offers a variety of similar products from different suppliers. Different suppliers have different pricing of products and also different times of delivery. Oberlo application enables you to choose a supplier with good ratings that will facilitate good and effective delivery of products to the customers. A drop shipper who chooses a good supplier will enable a site to have an amazing sale of a proposition.

- **Feature of automated pricing**

  Checking on the margin is a very crucial matter to focus on since it will determine the profits you make on the business. Oberlo application is able to automate the prices of bulk products according to the pricing rules set by the drop shipper.

- **Customization of product**

Oberlo application enables you to customize your products. Making your products look unique from other products creates an amazing display of the products to online customers. Products can be customized based on their descriptions, titles, and also their images.

- **Automatic update of product inventory**

The Oberlo software enables us to update the inventory of the products automatically. It helps in clearing products that are already out of stock instead of selling to the customers' stock that is not available. This helps your site to stay refreshed and updated building a good reputation for your site by the customers. It also saves you time instead of running and importing inventory reports.

- **Variant mapping**

This feature assists in merging similar products from different suppliers and separating the sizes and colors onto their own page.

- **ePacket delivery**

This feature enables us to cut down the long days of shipping of a product to customers. Long ago, the shipping of a product would normally take about two months. ePacket delivery enables a product to be shipped to the customer within four to nine days. This ePacket delivery has its own benefits, such as:

- ✓ Less shipping costs.
- ✓ Faster shipping of goods.
- ✓ Better retention of customers because of faster and cheaper shipping of their products.
- ✓ There is reduced responsibility due to ePacket delivery.
- ✓ Reduced risks involved.
- ✓ Reduced stress over loss of the products shipped since there is additional tracking of the products.
- ✓ Possible increase in sales due to the efficient shipping of the customer's goods.

Pros of the App

The advantages of the app include the following:

- Product importation from Aliexpress is secure and faster, with only just one click on the application.

- The application is simple to operate.

- The Oberlo app has a lot of resources. An instance is the Oberlo blog that provides guidelines to new store owners on how to set up their stores.

- There is the existence of the modern dashboard feature on the software with a user-friendly interface.

- Less effort is needed when using Oberlo software.

- Time is saved when doing the dropshipping business since the app simplifies the dropshipping business.

- Prices on the products are automated, increasing efficiency and effectiveness.

- Tracking of the shipments goods increases the security of the goods reducing the risks that arise during the shipment.

- The software ability to change on the suppliers of the goods makes the drop shipper be able to select the best supplier who will ensure effective shipment of the products ordered to the customers.

- It ensures fast delivery of shipment goods by the use of the packet filter. This promotes good customer service and massive retention of customers since the ordered goods are delivered on time, satisfying the customer's needs.

- The application ability to track the sales, monitoring the performance of a store, and the most selling product is able to be viewed at a glance.

Cons of the App

Oberlo application has various disadvantages:

- The software cannot run on standalone websites unless it is integrated with the Shopify store.

- The application only supports the Aliexpress platform.

- Products are normally added manually to the Shopify store.

Other Apps Used in Dropshipping

Other alternative applications that can be used in dropshipping include:

Dropship Connector

This is the best Oberlo alternative because the application as opposed to Aliexpress, it offers mostly European Union and United States products. This app is also able to automate the tracking of the sales and the workflow. Oberlo is not only available on Shopify but also on ShopBase. Dropship connector is a free app with no monthly fees and transaction fees required.

Features and Advantages of This App

- It's an app that automatically updates tracking numbers onto PayPal accounts for its users, making it a unique app.

- The app also automatically tracks orders made by the customers and fulfill them with just one click.

- Drop connectors can also change suppliers for your products by choosing qualified and reliable suppliers.

- You can set your own shipping rules based on the regions involved, which smoothens the operations by saving time and effort.

- Product inventory is auto-synced daily when they are adjustments made by the suppliers. This helps to avoid selling already sold stock to the customers. The effect of this feature makes customers always happy, promoting massive retention of the customers.

Spocket

Spocket is another alternative to Oberlo, which is highly rated. It is more advanced due to its possession of good quality suppliers who come from Europe and the US, unlike it is seen in Oberlo.

On the most basic plan, it is free to use Spocket. A merchant can add up 25 products to the store and be able to receive an unlimited number of orders from the products.

The pricing plans for Spocket include the basic plan, which is free with unlimited orders, and you can order up to 25 products, standard plan with the cost of $39.90 per month, and you can order up to 250 products plus all the things on the basic plan. The third plan is the professional plan with the cost of $99.90 per month with unlimited products plus all the features on the standard plan.

There are various features of Spocket application:

- Promotes a massive selection of inventory products

- Possess the discounted products and premium products

- Discounted products are the products with rates further with the original price Premium products; on the other hand, are the products associated with the paid plans. Premium products possess extra features that will enable customers to feel special, unlike those with discounted products.

- Shipping time is shortened because of the faster and efficient shipment of goods. Most of the time, it normally takes 2-5 business days.

- Update on the inventory products

- Spocket normally updates the stock available automatically to avoid riots and confusion in cases the merchants sell products that are already out of stock.

- Feature of shipment tracking numbers

- Email support feature

Spocket complies with certain standards on how to choose their suppliers which are:

- Application
  Suppliers need to apply in order to fit in the Spocket marketplace. The supplier whose products match up with the merchant's needs is the one most preferred.

- Interview
  Suppliers are called for an interview by the Spocket team. This is the part where Spocket is so keen to grasp some information about the sales and the history of the supplier. This has to happen to ensure that the supplier is a good fit for the merchants.

- Testing of products
  Spocket team orders products from the supplier's store to check on the quality of the goods, the packaging of the product inventory, and also the shipping duration of the goods. Factors like long shipping duration and poor

quality of products are not tolerated. Suppliers with this kind of factors fail to fit in the Spocket marketplace.

The performance of the suppliers who succeed to meet the standards above is normally monitored for the first two months

Advantages.

Spocket is an extraordinary application on its own.

- It has amazing discounts for dropshippers, at the range of 30-60%, contributing to definitely great profit margins.

- Spocket is available across all corners of the world.

- This app can also convert and configure the currency for your goods according to your Shopify store's currency since the default currency in Spocket is normally in USD.

- The app enables a merchant to customize its products according to their own preferences in terms of branding, description, pricing, and photos.

- Spocket has no upfront cost, no registration fees or details of credit card are required.

- No emergence of stock issues because the application automatically updates on the stock available.

- The shipping of the inventory stock is fast, reliable, and effortless.

- The processing of the orders is automated. The orders that are made on products are automatically sent to the Spocket suppliers making it effective other than manual procedures.

- You can get started so easily using the Spocket free plan, which charges no fees.

- Selling using Spocket is at ease. Selling can happen with one click. Orders can be fulfilled can also be made with one click.

- Spocket allows you to dropship the best products from a variety.

- The application allows merchants to test out products and suppliers so as to build efficient and effective businesses.

- Ensures effective selection of the suppliers who are qualified enough to smoothen the business operations by ensuring maximum customer satisfaction and good quality products.

- New suppliers are automatically added daily by the application.

Disadvantages

- Spocket products cannot be sold on some platforms such as Amazon, eBay, and Wish.

- There is the exclusion of taxes and customs duty on the products.

- Suppliers are only suited in the US and EU. The pricing of the products may, therefore, not be cheap.

Printful

Printful is another dropshipping application with a free pricing plan, no matter the number of your products and orders of your store. Its printing facilities are available in the USA, Latvia and also Mexico.

How does this app work?

Printful application normally provides you with products that you order, like, t-shirts and sweaters, and you are supposed to provide the designs to be made on the products. The application will print the designs for you and will automatically ship the products directly to the customers. There is no manual fulfillment of the orders, Printful will automatically fulfill the orders every time, and each and every detail saved online.

This application has its own advantages and disadvantages.

Advantages

- Printful does absolutely everything for you. All the shipping, fulfilling, and printing of products.

- The app has a wide variety of products to purchase from men, women, and kid's clothing, home and living products, and accessories.

- Customer orders are managed automatically to your Shopify store.

- Provides guidelines on the Frequently Asked Questions on how to set up a store.

- Assist in customizing dropshipped products by providing branding services.

- Tracks shipping for all products.

Disadvantages

- It has limited branding options. You cannot use your own branding options to customize your products.

- Some products, such as framed posters cannot be shipped to every country.

Mxed

Mxed is a dropshipping solution which is concerned with merchants who want to sell pop culture products such as Movie products to their customers. Most of the merchants have not been able to sell the products due to the stringent rules and policies.

How does it work?

Mxed application allows you to sell licensed pop culture products to your customers within your Shopify store, where customers will place orders on the products of preference. Mxed application will then fulfill and automatically ship the products directly to the customers.

Mxed consists of 3 pricing plans. The noob plan, which is free, for 10 products and up to 20 orders per month. The professional plan, which costs $50 per month, for 250 products, up to 500 orders per month. Lastly, there is the expert plan, which costs $99 per month for 500 products with unlimited orders.

The features of Mxed include the following:

- Offer a wide variety of licensed products. The popular licensed Mxed stock includes DC, Marvel, and Nickelodeon.

- Have an automatic dropshipping fulfillment. All orders made by the customers are automatically fulfilled by Mxed and shipped to the customers within 3-5 business days.

- Have an automatic update of inventory and pricing of products. You are able to know the sold-out stock and the one available for sale.

The advantages of this application include:

- Automatic pricing and update of the inventory.

- The application has direct integration with Shopify.

The disadvantages constitute the following:

- Mxed integrates only with the Shopify platform.

Modalyst

Modalyst is a platform that allows dropshipping business between merchants and suppliers to take place. The main aim of this application is to organize and maintain a variety of preferred premium products. It offers quick and reliable shipping to the US, Europe, and any big market globally.

The pricing tier of this platform include:

- The hobby plan, which is free of charge with a limit of 25 products.

- $35/month, which has the features of real-time data, pricing, and product descriptions.

- Its membership plan is yearly for $360 or either paid in installments of $35 per month.

The key features of modalyst include:

- Can easily add up to new suppliers

- Merchants pay for products after customers have ordered from the store

- No cost is incurred in adding products to your store

- Merchants can customize the details of the products according to their preference

Modalyst has the advantages of:

- Saving supplier's time other than wasting time searching for the right products.

- Faster and reliable shipment of goods to customers since the locations involved are the US and Europe other than overseas.

- No upfront stock costs are involved in using this platform.

- You are able to be informed when your products are out of stock.

- Availability of the free monthly plan for beginners

Disadvantages

Modalyst is an existing application with the following limitations:

- There may be varying shipping costs when each branding is independent.

- You need to upgrade to the pro plan and the business premium plan in order to access the network's suppliers.

- The process of placing an order is manual. A merchant needs to do it manually to pay for the order before being fulfilled by the supplier.

Gooten

This is a dropshipping platform that presents printed products that are on demand. A merchant is supposed to select the products according to preference, add some designs, and lastly, wait for Gooten to package and ship the products to customers. No fees are required, unlike it is seen on other platforms.

The advantages of this platform are:

- No charges incurred, neither monthly nor yearly.

- The shipment of goods occurs globally.

- It is simple and easy to use.

- It has great customer satisfaction due to the reliable shipment of goods.

- Produce goods of high quality

- There are automatic processing and fulfillment of orders to make customers happy.

It's a disadvantage that it provides no branding services.

Inventory Source

This is a dropshipping platform that connects your Shopify store with other supplier networks. It simplifies the dropshipping business and the inventory management process.

It has three pricing plans:

- A free account that views the policies and products of the supplier.

- An inventory sync account charges $50 per month with tools of huge feed management, ability to add customs, and automatic data upload

- A full sync account costs $150 per month, which supports automatic order processing and tracking of the shipment of goods.

Its advantages include:

- Automatic upload of data on the products.

- The application integrates with eBay, Amazon, and Walmart.

- There is an automatic processing of orders made by the customers.

- Have a direct connection with suppliers.

It has the following limitations:

- Fees are incurred monthly.

- The great features of this application are only available on the most expensive plan.

Chapter 5: The Suppliers Directory

Ever had the thought of purchasing goods and services online with no idea of how to get the right suppliers? The supplier's directory will guide you with tips on how to. A supplier's directory is a major list of wholesale suppliers planned by the market, which portrays and ensure legitimate suppliers. It aims to assist you in how to find the best suppliers for your goods and services.

The supplier's directory is for everyone and the points below are the reason why we use this directory:

- New entrepreneurs who are thinking of starting their businesses off.

- Individuals who are helplessly looking for product ideas

- Existing entrepreneurs looking for the best product to sell next

- Existing and established entrepreneurs looking for new products to add to their inventory.

- Entrepreneurs are looking for products they can dropship quickly to start off their business.

Why Use the Supplier's Directory?

It is very difficult to find high-quality suppliers due to the following reasons:

- Most of the legit and good quality suppliers do not know how to advertise themselves on the internet.

- Some suppliers who offer the dropshipping services fail to use keywords such as dropshipping making it difficult to be found by online users.

- Most suppliers offer dropshipping services to businesses they have totally no idea of.

The requirements needed in order to be connected with the dropshipping suppliers are as follows:

- An EIN number. This is a number for social insurance, especially in the USA, which is compulsory to have for a proper business set up.

- A resale permit. This certificate exempts you from paying the sales tax when reselling products to others through your customers will pay for the sales tax. The money paid is supposed to be sent to the State on an agreed schedule.

Before listing down the various dropshipping suppliers, let's dig deeper into the various ways on how to tell apart the legitimate suppliers and the fake ones. Many dropshippers fall into the fake suppliers ending up having poor performances and spending a lot.

Who Are the Best Suppliers to Use?

The following are the guidelines to follow on how to choose the right suppliers for your goods.

- Minimum Order Quantity. Suppliers with low minimum order quantity they are not the ideal ones. They will be no need for a dropshipper to buy inventory upfront.

- Quality of products. Working with a supplier with good quality of products is so crucial. This will retain more customers and satisfy them more.

- Fast and reliable shipping of products. Customers always love fast, efficient, and reliable shipment of goods. This will promote a positive attitude toward your products by the customers.

- Great communication skills. Working with a supplier with great communication skills is so important. A supplier who stays updated by replying to emails and updates you with the products available and out of stock helps you build a good reputation with the customers in the market.

- A wide selection of products. A drop-shipper who selects a supplier with a vast range of products has the potential of increasing sales by offering more products to the customers.

- Suppliers within the target market. Working with dropshipping suppliers within your target market is a privilege to your customers since their orders will be received on time, and taxes to be paid will be at least minimal.

- Choosing the right supplier. Selecting the right dropshipping supplier and not some sort of middleman enables you to get healthy profit margins.

- Return policy employed. Connect with suppliers who mention what their return policy is and how they handle it.

- Testing and product sample. Select a supplier who provides samples and permits testing of products. This will assure you, good products for your customers.

- Product branding. Dropshipping suppliers with the skill of providing different branding options like logo, packaging on the products normally attract more customers widening the market.

- Product uniqueness. Suppliers that offer unique products have high chances of well establishing your business to higher grounds.

Who Are the Non-Legitimate Dropshipping Suppliers to Shun From?

Most drop-shippers over time fall on fake suppliers' hands ending up losing a lot after all the struggle. Say no more; I have elaborated some factors for you to check out keenly. Below are some of the points:

- Minimum Order Quantity. Dropshipping suppliers who insist on payment of the minimum order quantity are the ones to avoid them quickly. Normally, drop-shippers don't go by the Minimum Order Quantity, and they also do not require an upfront payment.

- Outdated products. Updated and unique products are the ones that establish a business. Suppliers that offer outdated and common products are to be cut off since they will pull your business down.

- Low-quality products. Make sure the products your supplier is offering meets the standards for the good performance of the business.

- Slow and reliable shipping of products. Work with a dropshipping supplier who is ready to ship products effectively is able to ship goods in the shortest time possible. Delayed shipping of products annoys customers too much, resulting in too many complaints.

- Poor communication of supplier. Select a supplier who is so good at communication. Poor communication between them might result in same confusion, mismanagement, and fall of the business.

- Low-profit margins. Profit is so crucial for every business. Consider a supplier who understands the importance of it and who works harder for higher profit margins.

- Select suppliers who do not have outdated websites. Outdated websites will not allow automatic orders and will delay the shipment of goods.

- Supplier's inconvenience location. Suppliers who are so far away from the target market, like overseas, end up having paid high duties when shipping goods to the customers and consume a lot of shipping time.

How to Find Wholesale Dropshipping Suppliers?

Once you have an idea of how to tell real and non-legitimate suppliers apart, let us now elaborate on the various ways on how to find dropshipping suppliers.

- Contacting the manufacturer directly. This is mostly the advised approach to embrace, especially if you know the manufacturer of the type of brand or product you are handling. The manufacturer can lead you to an authorized distributor with the knowledge of the dropshipping program. On the other hand, if you have no idea of the manufacturer, you can look over online and see what you can get.

- Google searching. This approach is so difficult. Most of dropshipping suppliers have outdated websites. Use specific keywords when using this approach in order to fall under something useful.

It is normally tough to search for suppliers online, the supplier's directory, therefore, will simplify ways out in dropshipping.

Below is a list of various suppliers' directories. You should carefully take a look at building a better dropshipping business today.

- **Aliexpress**

Acts as the Chinese store of Amazon. Packages normally take 2-3 weeks to be delivered to the USA. No upfront costs needed to AliExpress. The downfall of AliExpress is that this business extends for another one month to get to the other parts of the world.

Its benefits include:

- Relatively cheap compared to other directories since there are no upfront costs.
- Has a robust selection of goods.
- Has many suppliers

- It can integrate easily with Shopify and others like Oberlo.

- **SalesHoo**

SalesHoo is an online directory suited in New Zealand and was founded in 2005. It has the largest selection of goods from various wholesalers all over the world. Comprises of around 1.6 million products from at least 800 suppliers. It offers a wide variety of goods, from clothes, accessories all over the world. To access this software, you need to pay a yearly payment of $67.

It has its own advantages which include:

- Wide variety of products of around 1.6 million.
- It has great customer support.

- Provide a lot of free resources to guide you on how to run a dropshipping business.

Its disadvantage is that it charges an upfront fee of $67.

- **Worldwide Brands**

Chris Malta, an eBay power seller, founded this directory in 1999. It is the oldest of the wholesale supplier's directory. Exceeds 10 million products with thousands of wholesalers. Its lifetime membership costs $299.

Suitable for most individuals making large orders.

Its advantages include:

- Has a database of about 1.8 million goods.
- Has good access to supplier's information and goods.

Limitations

- Its high fee of $299 is unsuitable for small businesses.

- **Dropship Direct**

This is a major directory with more than 900,000 products from 900 suppliers. It is well known for its backend data management system and its transparency. Uses PushList technology to customize the data feeds for various market hosts.

The pros include:

- Good customer support.
- Has one of the best back end management system since it uses PushList technology.

The disadvantages include:

- It is an expensive directory as compared to other directories.
- It offers a small range of products.

- **ESource**

eSource is an online directory suited in the United Kingdom. It has over 170,000 drop shippers. You need to create an account in order to get the company's listing. It is free to sign up if you are only buying the products. However, the cost is $20 per month, $50 for every six weeks, and $75 for every year.

The pros of this directory include:

- As dropshipping software, it has a lot to offer.
- Companies can be given the TradePass badge and be verified.

The downfall for eSource is that some members are charged for membership fees.

- **Wholesale Central**

This is a directory established in 1996. It has around 1400 suppliers with at least 740,000 products. It has no upfront fees;

This site makes reviews on suppliers to make sure they are legit and to be trusted. Wholesale central makes money by selling listings of suppliers to companies. It ensures strictly business to business operations and not consumers.

The advantages of Wholesale Central include:

- It has a wide range of suppliers.
- It is the largest supplier's directory.
- Good customer support

Its limitations are that:

- It is hectic to connect to the suppliers.
- Not suitable for beginners

- **Inventory Source**

Inventory Source is a dropshipping software with over 1 million products from 100 suppliers. Possesses a huge inventory and back end management system. You can export descriptions of products plus images to your site with just one click. Lacking a site is not an issue since inventory source will provide one for you.

One issue with this software is that it cannot bundle up orders from customers.

Its advantages are:

- Good customer service.
- Provide accessibility to integrated suppliers.

Its limitations are:

- The higher the number of suppliers, the higher the fees.
- Difficult to connect with the right suppliers.

- **Megagoods**

This is the directory to choose if you want to focus on video games and consumer electronics mainly. It is mainly suited in Los Angeles, in USA, with around 2000 products only. Some of the benefits of megagoods are:

- A customer has no idea the goods were sent by a third party.
- The site dropships the goods for you.
- It has a good shipping policy, megagoods tracks all shipments taking 1-2 days.
- Has an amazing return policy for electronics customers.
- A customer has a guarantee of 30 days of defects after the delivery of the goods.
- The fees are cheaper compared to other directories.

Some of its limitations include:

It does not offer a wide variety of goods; it only consumes electronics and video games.

- **Doba**

It is one of the largest dropship services suited in Utah, USA. Doba has exceeded two million products from around 200 suppliers. It has a very user-friendly UI. It has a management system for the stock, which alerts you in case you are running low on stock or any changes in the product description. The cost for the basic plan is $29 per month, which is costly compared to other directories.

Its benefits include:

- Integrates with Amazon, eBay, and Shopify using push list technology.
- Great customer support

Its pros include:

- It is costly, mostly for beginners.
- Unsuitable for less experienced drop-shippers.

Chapter 6: The Pricing Strategy

Dropshipping is an e-commerce plan that is trending in the current market. It is known to be very effective and requires minimum efforts. It will guarantee you maximum gains. It may seem too easy to operate, but it can be challenging if you do not effectively choose your prices. Your prices will rank you in a strategic position. The policy that you use for your process needs to be set out in a perfect manner.

Your only revenue when you are into drop shipping is simply computed. It is the supplier price and the price you set. You need to have a perfect balance between them so you will be enjoying the gains. The advice is always to be careful about how you price your items. This is what will break or make your business. There are guidelines that need to be followed in order to have the correct prices.

- When you are on the webstore looking for products, ensure that you avoid any cheap items. Most people think that when you go for cheaper products, you'll end up having bigger profits. That is not the case. Cheap products do not guarantee good gains. Make sure you have our personal standards, and your store needs to be aligned to a specific style. This will guarantee your success in the long run. If you think that pricing your products low will attract more customers, you should think again. They may end up thinking that your products are cheap, and the quality is low, and they may end up not buying your products. This is the reason why you do not lower your prices and you will have more customers coming to your store.

- When pricing your products on dropshipping, ensure that you maintain a high price. This can be at the start of your business. When you become comfortable, and you've maintained your loyalty customers for a while, you should start offering discounts, coupons and offers. If you have any special discounts, do not be afraid to offer it to your customers. When you have a variation in your prices, you'll be able to attract more customers. And this will also improve your pricing approaches and methods. You will also improve your online presence.

- Another better strategy in setting your prices is when you choose products that do not require any shipping cost. This is because most of the customers prefer them. And when you are pricing, you'll end up pricing lower as compared to your competitor. The reason being, the buying price will be lower, and you will make higher gains. This will put you in a competitive edge and advantage. When you need to pay shipping charges, this means that you'll pay a higher price. And when you pay a higher price for your products, you'll end up getting a higher selling price, the consequences of that are you'll start losing your customer. When your revenue is reduced, that means you'll not be able to achieve your business goal, which is making greater returns. A good approach in dropshipping is to offer to your customers products, at zero shipping cost.

- Do some exploration before determining your prices. This is considered an important thing to do. You need to diversify, do not be stagnant in the traditional ways. When you want to know the new trends available, you need to have a keen eye and good taste. This will be one way of being ahead of your competitors. When you stick to an old plan, chances are that it will not be beneficial. When you are looking for a line for your products, you need to diversify all your choices. When you get attractive and quality products, it will be easy for your customers to make their purchase decision. They will like what they see, and this will help in increasing your sales and profits. Ensure you offer them a variety to choose from. When your customers are guaranteed of quality products, fair prices, and a wide variety, they will not have any issue buying from you and they will also have constant purchases, and even referrals.

- Ensure when you are setting your prices, you also deal with returns. When you get your goods returned, it can be depressing as a dropshipper even though there could be reasons that you cannot control. When managing your returns, it can also act as a way to know more about your customers. So, you can take it as a way to learn more and use that as a step to your success. The first step to maintain your sales is always making your customers happy. When such a scenario happens, do not panic or get stressed. All you need to do is pay attention to what the situation is and not just the problem and when your customers are happy, you'll be able to make regulars, and you could give them a good price. That will end in determining the prices for the products to be dropshipped.

- You need to be flexible when it comes to determining prices. You need to adapt and embrace change. It is important to have a change in your items, the cost price, and the approaches that you use. Ensure that your business venture is flexible enough. Always have price assessment and make adjustments where necessary in regard to your market. Make sure you are ahead of your competitors and look at how they operate.

- When you are planning on how to determine your prices, ensure your stocks are appealing and will attract your customers. When your products have such features, they will be irresistible, and it will not be hard for customers to find them. You need to go for products that are considered trendy, and that will be fast-moving when online. And when you get quality products and fair prices, your customer will be ready to pay any price for that. That will be to your advantage.

- The best customer support is the most important thing in your business operations. Most online business is known to provide affordable products, but their customer support is wanting. Most suppliers think that offering fair prices, is the way to get customers. The real reason is offering the best customer support. This is the key element in getting new customers and maintaining them. Always maintain your business venture by listening to what the customers say. Pay attention to their needs, the complaints they have, and what they demand. When your customers believe in you, they will trust you and when that does happen, they will be willing to pay whatever price you indicate for your products and services that you are offering. They will be assured that you will be reliable and be there for them when they need you.

- There is a psychological element to pricing. Most of the customers will prefer prices that have last numbers that are in odd characters. When the price is indicated as

$10.99, most customers will translate it to $10. It is considered a normal thing, but in a real sense, it is weird. It is something that you can try out in your business. And analyze your customer's reactions, and if it picks well, you can apply it to your dropshipping business. That will guarantee you better sales if your customers end up adapting it.

How to Compare Prices Using the MAP Technique

Manufacturers get their products to the customers through different retailers. The main setback is that customers will get the same products at a higher price. This price will be higher as compared to buying from a wholesaler. So, the retailers will have issues and a disadvantage when competing with wholesalers in regard to selling their products.

For that reason, it is advisable to stick to the minimum advertised price commonly known as MAP. This is the minimum cost that brands and retailers can use to advertise and sell. You should know that this will not limit the way you'll price your products. And that means it will not affect your sales. The prices agreed will be based on the negotiations you'll have with your manufacturers. The price is always set more than the minimum advertised price.

When items are sold at the lowest price as compared to the minimum advertised price, this can affect the market for the retailers. This will end up affecting your brand name, appearance, and even your profit margin. The importance of the minimum advertised price is that any retailer is able to sell its products. This means, when a product sells below the MAP, your sales as a retailer will increase. This strategy helps in preventing retailers from looking for shortcuts in order to be popular in the market. This mainly happens to retailers that have experience in the online business. When there is stiff competition, the prices seem to go down — and hence resulting in market imbalance.

MAP strategy is used in price comparison and in different parts of the world. They are named in different terms but mean the same. It is mostly used in advertising by a manufacturing company, and they will tell the retailers which prices they should use when advertising their products. The MAP policy is very strict and should not be violated. A good example is when a manufacturer puts the price at $50. The retailer is supposed to price at that level, nothing more and nothing less. If it's not at that price, they are considered to have violated the policy for the MAP strategy. Another version will be when the stores offer a coupon to either their new or existing customers. That will reduce the cost price of the product. What happens after they add it to their cart, but this does not mean that they have violated the map policy that was set by the manufacturer.

When price comparison sites do their analysis, they always pick stores that have the lowest cost on their products. This will entice more customers to your store, especially customers who are very sensitive to prices. This is beneficial since it will lead to more sales brought about by an advertisement that is considered indirect. This example is relevant to show that you can get customers through indirect advertisements and not necessarily enticing customers with low prices; thereafter, lowering the price when the customer buys a specific product quantity from them.

How to Know the Profitable Products for Dropshipping Based on Regions

When you decide to engage in dropshipping, ensure that you look for products that are attractive and easy to sell. Do not be in a hurry to compete with the biggest e-commerce, like Amazon and eBay. If you take that bold step to compete, they might affect your business by competing with them.

- Avoid any products that are very popular, and this is because common items tend to be very competitive. This will end up reducing your profit. Always look for a product that is unique and then change it into a unique product that will fit your personality. The next step is to look for retailers and compete against them. This should be based on the prices, product choice, product availability, and selection. An example of a common item to sell are children's play toys and items of clothing. They are considered common, but again, they sell faster so, the idea is to have a competitive advantage over the products. Look for something unique and set yourself above your competitors.

- Look for products that are less popular and from a niche that is also not common. That will bring about less competition. When you are able to access your set niche market, then that is the best product to sell. There are different items that are not very popular and will make up for the best products to sell. These are products that you need to be very observant in order to analyze the best niche markets for your products. There are products that are less popular and very marketable. These include vests that are bulletproof, and equipment used for diving. This is a special niche, and not many people will want them. But that does not mean that they are not needed.

- Look for the right price for your product niche. The price should be the best for your niche. Like if your niche is clothing, price as per the customer's usage. If it's a shirt that is the high end, it can be priced higher as compared to an everyday shirt. You need to do comprehensive research and know how to do your pricing.

- Always look for products that offer a great profit margin, at least a 30% profit. When you go for items that are very popular, chances are you will end up getting lower profits. This is because you will be forced to sell at lower prices in order to manage sales and beat the competition. You need to research more to get items that will offer good profits.

- Products from reliable suppliers and with a good reputation tend to sell faster. Look for suppliers that are well-vetted, and you'll have peace of mind that they will deliver. If that is not possible, look for suppliers who specialize in drop shipping only. This will enable you not to affect the relationship you have with your suppliers. Look for dropshipping suppliers who understand the model well. Suppliers are a vital part of the dropshipping process since they provide the products.

- Ensure to refer to your personal exposure and experience on the products. This will be the knowledge that you have on the product to share with your customers. A product that you have a personal touch and experience will be easy to sell. You'll have a competitive advantage over your competitors. You can even clearly explain all the technical and complicated parts of the product. And all the uses that the product offers, and this will make your sale process easy. For instance, if you are an expert in drilling, you can easily sell the equipment and show the customers how to use the machine or equipment. You will be in a position to help them choose the best for their work. That will be an added advantage to you and selling will be an easy process.

The Trends That Help to Know Growth and Decline

The trends are what we use to calculate the growth and the decline of our products and what determines the profit or loss it is the flow and the movement of the prices in the chart. The trend is used primarily to give us an overall situation of the market, and it is supposed to predict the near future.

The bull market happens when there is a rise in prices it means that the price of the product rises too. The general, during that market, the emotion experienced is pessimism. When most of the participants are bearish, their feeling will then change to being hopeful and optimistic as the price is going down which it can lead to a recession period. There was an analysis that was done, and the bull market had an average return of more than 450% in eight years and the annual profits were above 30%.

As for the bear market, it means that, there is a decline in the price for a period of time. Trends are good at helping you to understand when your product is in their declining life or viceversa.

How to Manage Your Competitors and Generate Traffic (SEO)

When in any business, you need to know about your competitors and be above them. Always stay ahead of them and get a good position in the market. There are different ways that can help to beat your competitors. You need to be aggressive in that because the competition is predictable in any market environment.

- Research and know about your customer's problems and offer a solution. There are different ways of doing that. You can start by asking questions, and you'll be able to know what their problem is. Ask some open-ended questions, and this will be used as a guide. The main reason for doing all that is to offer a solution to what they need, instead of selling to them what you are selling and meet their needs and demands first. When you meet all their needs, it will be easier to sell since your competitors are also not offering that.

- To be competitive, you need to choose your own product niche, and you'll have more business opportunities. When you choose a niche that already has several suppliers, it will be hard to penetrate into the market and to expand your business. You need to provide something that is unique in order for your customers to be able to buy from you; this will end up in reducing competition. You can create a story and have your own product niche.

- You will be able to customize your products and align them with your lifestyle. It will not be like the normal products that your competitors are offering. You'll be able to generate traffic to your products and hence more sales. You can use free photography to create awareness and promote your products and it will help with your presence on social media platforms. It will be easier for your customers to target as long as you are reliable. Start out with local platforms that are easily targeted by your customers.

- There is a need to ensure that your pricing strategy is correct. You need to practice the correct marketing psychology to have the best pricing approach. You are advised to know your competition before setting the price. The next step is to know who among your competitors are giving the best money value. And lastly, the price should be on a standard level and a competitive edge.

- When you are setting your price, lowering the cost will not mean that you are effective. You will still be able to be ahead of your competitors. There are market segments that you need to know; lower, middle, and upper. The first step is knowing the product class that you want to target. When you do that, you will be able to set your price that is comfortable with your customers easily.

- Be innovative. Try and know what is trendy and be innovative. Plan your products and prices as per customers' needs. Ensure the products and services that you're offering are innovative and up to the challenge of the risky business environment, like adding more capability features in all your business needs. A good example is how Blackberry was taken out of the market for not being innovative. Most of their phones were outdated. When your competitors are innovative, you also need to style up. Innovation is a regular thing, and there are new products each time. You need to keep up with your competitor's pace.

- All customers will always love excellent customer care. Ensure you improve your customer care. Customers will also yearn for good customer support. When your customers are delighted with your service, they will be constant customers. They will even make referrals to other people. Ensure that when you are recruiting, get an experienced workforce, staff who understand the products and services. Keep training them all the time.

They should be patient and offer answers to customers' questions.

- They should greet the customers when they get to your store. They should have a smile when addressing them and extend gratitude. Always boost their team spirit and be a team player. Have a reward system for the performing staff, and they will need the motivation to be able to have a good performance. The customer support team is supposed to have respect and have courtesy. They should be able to respond to customers' questions and be able to solve problems. They need to be approachable and be able to always ask for customers' feedback. There is a need to set your brand. This will enable you to outperform your competitors, and this will be in the form of the product price, great customer care, and best product quality. And Finally, this will enable you to service your customers above your competitors, hence retaining them, have more sales, and more profits.

Chapter 7: Dropshipping and Amazon

The Pros and Cons of using an Individual Online Store to Drop Ship

What is Amazon?

Do you know what Amazon is all about? Amazon is a multinational technology company suited in Seattle, Washington. It is famously known for cloud computing services, e-commerce, and artificial intelligence. Jeff Bezos founded the Amazon business back on 5th July 1994 at Bellevue, Washington, in the United States. The name Amazon was chosen by Bezos because it began with the first alphabetical letter, and it was associated with the South American river. Amazon logo was constructed to represent the smile that will be drawn on customer's faces when they purchase anything from the website, and the logo also shows an arrow that connects letter A to Z to symbolize that Amazon website sells everything from A to Z.

It is originally known for the sale of books, which later on decided to sell electronics, music, furniture, software, jewelry, and apparel. In 2002, Amazon company introduced Amazon Web Services (AWS) that gave information on the internet and provided statistics to the software developers and economists. There was an expansion of the Amazon web services in 2006, leading to the introduction of the Elastic Compute Cloud that rented computer processing power in large and small amounts. Simple Storage Service was also introduced in the same year that rented data storage all over the internet. Millions of customers (individuals, institutions, and the government) trust the Amazon Web Services so as to power their start-ups and organizations and become more efficient.

This e-commerce company has half a million employees. Back in October 2017, Amazon announced it had 541,900 employees, an increase from the previous year. The average hourly wage for a full- time employee in fulfillment centers, which includes stock and cash, is over 15$/hour. There are about 80,000 sellers, developers, and authors that normally use the amazon platforms in the State alone.

The amount of revenue that Amazon normally yields is so amazing. The company's revenue in 2018 was more than $232 billion. Amazon has acquired companies such as Zappos, Audible, and Graphiq. Amazon subsidiaries include Ring, Whole Foods market, and IMDb.

How to Dropship on Amazon

Many online users would love purchasing goods from different parts of the world using various e-commerce websites but wonder how the goods will reach them, and this is where dropshipping comes in handy. Dropshipping is a supply management method where the retailer does not store the stock but rather transfers the customer's orders and the shipment details to the manufacturer who will supply the goods directly to the customer. Product manufacturers have the responsibility of manufacturing and maintaining the goods while drop shippers can set the prices of the goods.

Amazon Dropshipping is so legal and has various benefits which include:

- For a successful dropshipping business, only a few skills are needed. For a drop shipper to succeed, it is supposed to be excellent in marketing, possess great administrative tasks and customer service. Excellent marketing skills attract more customers from wide social platforms. On the administrative side, drop shippers can schedule themselves on how to pay for taxes and expenses and also on how to process orders made by different customers. Drop shippers with excellent customer service are able to retain more existing customers by providing positive relationships with them.

- Another benefit of dropshipping is that it has lower start-up costs. Drop shipper purchases a product only after an order is placed. There are no warehouse costs for goods. Amazon sellers prefer making their products satisfied by amazon to paying for the warehouse costs. Hiring employees to control the shipping of goods is not necessary for a drop shipper. The only costs incurred are advertising costs and website development and maintenance.

- Amazon has around 300 million active users. Thus, making drop shippers have a large audience to sell to. Selling the right goods at the right price can attract new customers giving you a chance to connect with many new customers from diverse demographics.

- Another benefit is that you can test products easily by running ads on them and see the products that convert best since you don't purchase inventory.

As you have already seen the advantages of dropshipping on Amazon above, it is necessary to comply with the steps below in order to be engaged in this exercise. The steps are in the following order:

- Linking up with the supplier so as to list their products on Amazon having the surety that the supplier is willing to ship the goods directly to the customer, so you won't have the need to do that.

- Creating listings and selling the products, ensuring the money paid by the consumer, cover both the shipping and retail costs.

- Handing over the collected money to the supplier, which is not 100% of the money from the consumer. You will be expected to wait for your next sale as the shipping of the product of the consumer is done by the supplier.

Dropshipping on Amazon is allowed as long as you comply with the following requirements:

- Become the one selling the record of your products.

- Make sure you introduce yourself as the one selling the products. Identify yourself on the packing slips, external packagings, and of course, on the invoices.

- Remove all the packing slips, invoices, and external packaging, identifying a third person drop shipper.

- Comply with the policies of the Amazon business and also the terms of the seller's agreement.

- Have the responsibility for processing and accepting customer returns for your products.

Failure to fulfill the requirements above may lead to suspension of your selling privileges on Amazon.

Amazon dropshipping tools may include the following:

- Merchant words tool to view keywords and their data.

- Shopify tool to track your inventory.

- Feed check tool to view all the reviews of our products in one place. This enables a drop shipper to monitor competitor's products and provide better customer services.

- Sellery tool assists in carrying pricing experiments to stay competitive.

- Feedback express tool to help end up with positive ratings on the Amazon website, be able also to get rid of the negative reviews, and blacklist consumers who frequently leave bad reviews.

Dropshipping on Amazon has its own advantages and disadvantages.

Pros

- Little or no capital outlay required since sellers miss out on the process of ordering, warehousing, and shipping of the inventory.

- Advantageous for sellers who deal with larger items. Larger products are a high cost to ship and store.

- Dropshipping on amazon gives you wide access to the audience; thus, fewer marketing skills are required.

- Dropshipping redistributes focus on sellers freeing up their time since they do not actively participate in the process and are able to focus more on marketing.

Cons

- The relationship between the seller and the consumer may be so poor because the sellers are not involved in the shipment of the goods ordered by the consumer.
- Amazon allows dropping shippers to make sales on the Amazon website using the FBA (Fulfillment by Amazon) program by Amazon and no other programs such as Oberlo.
- You expose your sales data when using the Amazon platform since Amazon s normally able to see the products that sell best and use the data to build themselves.
- No customization can be done on the products since Amazon is the one under control of the product's marketing and branding.

How to Dropship on eBay

How well do you know the eBay business? eBay is an e-commerce company suited in San Jose, California, which enables consumers to buy and sell items daily using the eBay website. Pierre Omidyar founded eBay on the date 3rd September back in 1995. The business has this website concerned with online sales and purchases which operates worldwide.

Anything can be auctioned on the eBay website as long as it is legal and complies with eBay policies. Millions of items are purchased and sold daily on eBay. The items may include domain names, vehicles, computers, appliances, clothes, décor, furnishings, and equipment. The categories of items that are prohibited on eBay include witchcraft services, tobacco, alcohol, body organs, drugs, souls and ghosts, ivory products, police and emergency services, fortune-telling services, and many others.

eBay, as a visible online market, has attracted wide various career fields, such as the computer information system researchers and economists. Computer information system researchers see eBay as a platform for big data since it processes around 50 petabytes of data per day. The economists also study the sales and purchase behavior and compare them with the theoretical findings.

Did you know that eBay is the 10th world largest company by revenue? The value of market capitalization of eBay is over US$27.2 billion back in October 2018. It charges no fee to buyers, unlike the sellers who are charged a fee for product listing and another fee when they sell their products.

How Does Dropshipping Work on eBay?

Dropshipping is allowed on eBay as long as the delivery is done within 30 days of the end of the product's listing. Also, you have to ensure not to drop ship from another retail marketplace like Amazon. A seller that drop-ship from other retail marketplace is suspended or lowered his ratings. Drop shippers on eBay are fully responsible for the quality and the shipping of the products. Anyone with an eBay seller's account can be an eBay drop shipper.

The following are the tips of becoming a successful eBay drop shipper:

- Deciding on the products you want to put on sales.

- Sourcing the products, you have chosen from a wholesaler who will guarantee you efficient and reliable shipping.

- Have a large volume of sales for huge returns.

- Have excellent marketing skills and reasonable pricing on the products to ensure maximum profits.

- Once the sales of the products listed begin rising, you should create an amazing reputation to maintain your customers and also try to deal accordingly with the matters that may arise.

Advantages and Limitations of Dropshipping on eBay

Everything has its own pros and cons. The following are the pros and cons of dropshipping on eBay:

Pros

- It is so simple and easy. There is no need to have a blog or a warehouse for storing your products. You only need to create an account and fill in your listings.

- Less marketing times. eBay is recognized by millions of online users; therefore, dropshipping on eBay saves time and marketing costs.

Cons

- Dropshipping on eBay requires one to purchase huge stock and pay listing fees, increasing your costs unless you have a manufacturer who will permit you to sell individual products.

- The fee for product listing on eBay is too high, and you are supposed to pay for the fee, yet you are not guaranteed if the product will be purchased. This leads to high business risks.

- There is no long-term relationship built with customers. A drop-shipper on eBay cannot secure a customer base for the products, and therefore ends up helping eBay grow other than your own business.

- There is no customization of products on eBay. All marketing and branding of the products are under the control of eBay.

Dropshipping with your Own Store

Dropshipping, as we have earlier stated, is a supply management process that involves 3 participants; customers, sellers, and the suppliers. A customer places an order of the product they want available on the supplier's website, the seller processes the order and the shipment details of the customer to the dropship supplier, and then the dropship supplier is the one responsible for packing and shipping the product directly to the customer.

How Do I Start to Dropshipping My Own Store?

It's very simple. Below are the steps to follow on how to drop-ship your own store:

Logistics

- Choose and register your business name as required.

- Decide on your business structure that you best prefer. Either a sole proprietorship form of business or partnership one.

- Acquire your business permit or license from the respective local government or state.

Identify a market.

For a successful business, you need to identify a target market that is different and unique from your competitors. Sell something that best interest you and which is easier to know. You then supposed to start with a small proportion of people within your target market and satisfy their needs. Study what and do much research on what the people are mostly engaged in. Try evaluating the profits you will make with low dropshipping margins.

Find a supplier.

Once you are satisfied with the target market, it's now the time to look for a dedicated drop-ship supplier who will be responsible for selling your products. Look for a supplier who is experienced with the dropshipping business, has good customer service with good reviews. Also consider suppliers who are efficient, reliable so as not to lose customers. Find suppliers that charge affordable fees since dropshipping margins are so low.

Build your website.

After finding a target market and a supplier for your goods, you obviously need a place to sell your products. You can create a personal website from scratch using an e-commerce platform.

Creating the business on an e-commerce platform is quite easy but comes with its own disadvantages. E-commerce marketplace like eBay and Amazon will limit your independence by charging fees on every sale you make, and you will not have control over the marketing, branding, and design of your own store according to their terms and conditions.

Creating your own e-commerce website is the best option. Given the different features of the e-commerce website by the website providers, you can customize your website according to your own preferences to increase marketing of the online store.

Market the website.

Make an effort to market your website in different ways to reach more audiences. You can market your website in different forms.

Use of email marketing to feed your customers each week with new sales arrivals.

Use of ads on Facebook, Twitter, and google to reach to your target audience.

Sources of Finance for Dropshipping My Own Store

The cost of starting a dropshipping business for your store is not that simple. You require finances for the marketing costs, for payment for the shipping charges and also for the e-commerce website. The finances can be acquired from different sources such as loan borrowing from different loan vendors which will help to pay for the expenses that may arise, and even applying for e-commerce grants which are free money though you have to wait for a lengthy period of time.

Pros and Cons of Using an Individual Online Store to Dropship

The pros of using an individual online store are that:

- A business owner can control the inventory according to the needs of the customers and does not need to depend on the third-party vendor, unlike it is seen on dropshipping.

- High-profit margins as compared to dropship since you deal with a high volume of inventory.

- Low risks may be involved in the business since you are dealing directly with the third parties.

The cons of using an individual online store to dropship include:

- A high initial cash outlay is required since business owners need to have a huge volume of inventory.

- It is expensive since the owner requires a large workspace to store the large volume of products in a warehouse.

Chapter 8: Supply Management and Customer Care

How to Manage Stock

All businesses should have an idea of how to manage their stock. Stock is the heart of the company. The act of ordering products, storing, tracking, and controlling the products is what it's defined as Stock management.

If there is poor management of your stock, there is a risk in your overall revenue for your business.

What is your stock management plan? What system can you use to manage your stock? Have you ever lost sales due to not stocking the item the customer was looking to buy? Did you stock too many items, and you ended up not selling them? All this question is crucial, to be able to check out if you are on the right track with how you do your stock management.

In this guide, we will go through ways to manage your stock, the available software you can use in your business to manage your inventory, the benefit of having a good stock management system and, mistakes to avoid during stock managing.

What is Stock Management: By understanding what stock management means, you will be able to know what is required of you. Having the right item, with the right quantity and at the perfect timet when it is needed. It is the simplest explanation of what stock management means. When implemented correctly, the business will increase its revenue and avoid having too much stock. By reducing excess inventory, it will reduce the total cost. Also, the business will be able to control stock-taking, thus the smooth running of your business.

Techniques of Stock Management: Every business has a different system on how they do their stock management. But regardless of this, the methods will help you improve your stock management.

Set par levels are the levels you set for your product. The minimum number of the product to have in your store at a given time. When that level drops, you know it's time to restock.

First-In-First-Out (FIFO): FIFO means the oldest products get to be sold first before the new products are sold. It is imperative, mainly, if you deal with perishable goods to avoid spoilage.

Have a Contingency Plan: There are many issues that can pop up concerning stock management. These issues can affect unprepared businesses. These issues include Sales spike unexpectedly, which can cause oversell of your stock — running out of cash flow and not being able to pay for products that you need. Lack of warehouse space. Miscalculation ending up with fewer products than you need.

Suppliers are running out of products. Suppliers discontinue a particular product without prior notification. Slow-moving products that take up all your storage space. It's not a matter of if problems arise, but when.

Know what your risks are and have a contingency plan. What are the steps you will take to sort out the problem? How will this be an impact on the rest of your business?

Built relationship: Have the best work relationship with your suppliers. It will come in handy when you want to return an item, exchanging a slow-selling item with a fast-moving item.

Regular auditing: You will be getting a report about the products from your software, but it's sometimes essential to physically go and check the products. It will help you to see if the numbers of the warehouse match the numbers from the software.

Consider dropshipping: Dropshipping is the best technique for stock management.

Prioritize with ABC: Some products require more attention than the other. By using the ABC analysis, you can separate products that require more attention than the others. You can categories them into three: High, moderate, and low-value products.

Accurate forecasting: The most significant part of good stock management is accurately predicting product demand. Make no mistake; it's tough to do it. There are many unexpected outcomes, and you can never predict what is going to happen, but you can be able to try at least to predict. Here are a few things to help you project your future sales: The current shift in the market, year's growth rate, the economy, planned adverts, and upcoming promotions. When you get more exposure in the business and more experience, you will be able to recognize more accurate forecasts to help you out, be sure to include them in your business.

List of Free Software to Help You with Stock Management

inFlow Inventory: This software suits all businesses. Can manage 100 products.

Odoo: It is an EPR tool, but it can also be used for stock management.

Sortly Pro: Cloud-based stock management tool for all businesses.

ZhenHub: Cloud-based stock management and logistics tool.

Zoho Inventory: Cloud-based stock management and warehouse tool.

There are many benefits of Stock Management. Here are the top 5 benefits:

- It increases the efficiency and productivity of your business.

- It creates more organization in your business.

- It saves you money and time.

- It improves accuracy, thus helping in preventing product shortage.

- By meeting your customer's demands efficiently, it will increase customer turnout.

How to Find Suppliers

It is much easier to find the supplier you need if you know which products you need. Here are some of the tips for finding a supplier:

- Understanding the distribution channels- By understanding your distribution channels, you can be able to know where you fit in the distribution channel. You will be able to find the right supplier fit for your business.

- You can begin with the manufacturer- Why not start with the source? By getting your products from the manufacturer reduces the product cost. But if the manufacturer is not able to supply the products directly to you, you can ask for a list of the distributors he supplies. This way, you can be able to get a great product and at a reduced price. It can increase your competitiveness in the job market.

- You can also use Google- Try to search for suppliers on Google. You can start your research with some Keywords. Find different suppliers and compare prices.

- Try local suppliers- You can reduce your shipping cost and the time it takes to get your order.

- Joining forums and other professional networks- By networking with other retailers to find the best suppliers for your products.

- Don't be afraid to make mistakes- Your first supplier may not be your long-term supplier. Your aim here is to ship your first product and make a profit. Then you can try other suppliers as you continue to learn in the industry.

How to Offer Great Customer Care

When you provide great customer service, you create loyal customers for life. And these customers will refer their friends and families. What experience does your customer have when they visit your website? What do they think about your store? What can you do to improve? These are questions you should ask yourself as they will guide you in providing the best customer service. Here are some tips to help you offer the best customer service:

- Know the products you sell. Learn all the common questions the customer asks. And their perfect answers for better customer satisfaction.

- Always be friendly. Greet your customer with a smile. Make them feel welcomed and appreciated. When you are on the phone with the customer, have a pleasant voice so that they can feel you are there to assist them. Be genuinely friendly with a smile.

- By simply saying, Thank you. Gratitude goes a long way by saying, thank you after every transaction is an excellent way of starting the best customer relationship.

- Offer more training to your staff on how to interact with the customers. Provide your team with the tools to be able to handle all customer issues, thus providing the best customer experience.

- Listening- This is the secret of customer service. Listen to your customer and what they want, so as to improve your customer service.

- Be responsive. Always respond to your customers when they have a question about a product, when they have an issue with the product they ordered, or when they want to find out more about the other products you sell.

- Request for feedback. After a sale, you can ask your customers for feedback. You can offer a customer survey or a questionnaire on your website that the customers can answer after they have made an order.

- Use the feedback you receive. Review the feedback you receive, improve on areas that had the issues, and make changes to your business.

Customer service should always be updated with the customer's issues and I assure you will constantly improve your business.

How to Avoid Mistakes in Supply

When the cost of your supply decreases, the profit margins increase. Once you master your supply chain, you will be able to cut costs. Here are some of the common mistakes in supply and how to avoid them:

- Absence of Supply chain transparency – The key to maximum efficiency is end-to-end supply chain visibility. You can make more educated decisions by mapping your business process from concept to customer.

- Disregarding supply chain data – In every stage of your business, all data is crucial, from your inventory quantity to the profit margins. To make better business decisions, you must utilize all of the supply chain data.

- Not planning ahead – The key to running a smooth business has a risk plan in place. When a problem in supply arises, you will be able to shield your customers from being affected.

- Having too many suppliers – The phrase "too many cooks in the kitchen." applies here. Having too many suppliers can cause complications. Research and find the right balance.

- Poor Customer service – The key to your business success is the supplier and the customer. Create a productive relationship with them to benefit your company. Your supply chain will be better if our relationship with them is better.

- Adhering to paper process – A mistake most businesses make is failing to utilize technology and focusing on inefficient paper-based workflow. Most Small businesses prefer keeping things simple. It can have a negative impact on the misplacement of documents. It can generate efficiency if you digitize your information and storage. There is simple and useful software you can use;

you don't need to buy expensive, complicated software for your paper trail. This will help save money and the environment as you will be eliminating the paper-based process.

- Poor housekeeping – Littered aisles, messy docking are all signs of a warehouse that does not receive much love. It might cause a safety risk. Without proper warehouse housekeeping, it will result in warehouse inefficiency. It will restrict the smooth flow of goods in your warehouse. You can avoid this by having a strict regime of housekeeping.

How to Handle Shipping and Fraud Issues

Managing your online store's shipping ensures that you are making the right profit margins, and you aren't leaving money off the table or risking the success of your business by charging too little. By having a well-planned shipping strategy for your online store, all the staff involved in the shipping process can be aware of what's going on, to ensure the smooth running of the shipping process and the business.

There are three most important considerations in shipping:

- **The Product Size and Weight**

What's the difference in size and weight? The first of these, product size and weight, is easier to get your head around and has the most prominent effects on how to approach it. It can have the most significant impact on your shipping rates and bring better returns on your investments.

- **Shipping Destinations**

Where is your shipping destination? Domestic or International? The shipping destination is also as essential as product size and weight. For domestic shipping, a flat rate or free shipping option can be possible.

- **Shipping Options**

What are the best shipping carriers for your unique products? Choosing the right shipping carrier, you will be able to please your customers and save on shipping costs. In major cities, there are local shipping carriers who are affordable and offers quick delivery to your customer. As compared to the big shipping carries who might have high shipping costs.

There are shipping issues businesses face, and it can be a challenging task to meet the customer's requirements and to ship their products on time. Even by offering excellent five-star services, the shipping process might affect your efforts.

Consequences of unexpected issues can delay your future orders. In search of a solution, most business owners end up spending money on things that are not unnecessary and taking the wrong solution at the last moment.

This eventually will lead to wasting a lot of time. You should instead implement activities and technologies that are simple and easy to acquire. By doing this, you will have saved on shipping issues and you will have had more time to focus on the order fulfillment process and customer support.

These will give you confidence when shipping bigger orders in the future. By listing the possible issues here, it can help you prepare better. Here are some of the shipping issues and possible solutions to guide you:

- **Delay in Delivery**

It is the most common issue in shipping. There are many reasons that can cause a delay. To make things simpler, I have classified them into two forms. Internal delays and external delays.

Internals can be controlled if you know how to handle them. For example, when shipping items to international borders, you have to make sure that you have the right customs documentations. Having incorrect documentation can lead to a license issue, and it can lead to shipping being led by the customs. If you handle perishable products, then indicate on the packaging to avoid problems.

External issues are caused by factors like bad weather, the delivery truck breaking down, and heavy traffic. You can completely overcome these external issues in informing your customers about the delay.

- **Inaccurate Tracking Information**

The computer generates the tracking number and assigned to the right orders. But most businesses do this process manually and print the shipping labels. By making this process manual, the risk of human error is high. One of the common issue due to wrong shipping information is, items delivered to the incorrect address. It can be bad for both the business owner and the customer.

- **Delivery Refusal by the Customer**

The customer can refuse to pay the pending order amount and request to return the item. Here are some of the common reasons – the customer made the wrong purchase, damaged item delivered, or the customer doesn't want the item anymore.

Managing returns can be a challenge, getting the order back, unpacking, and returning the item to inventory. It can cost you more time and money. Returns should be avoided at all times.

- **Handling Damaged Item during Shipment**

The customer may request you to repair their damaged item so they will ship the item back to you. So, the customer will have to initiate the shipping process. The customer may not want to be compliant with this, and it is not a good practice.

Luckily, there are some shipping plugins you can use which offer return label features. The business owner can return the shipping request to the shipping company. The shipping company approves your claim, and the business owner will pay for charges incurred.

Then the customer needs to send the item back to the shipping agent, and the shipping carrier will send the item back to the warehouse or the repair center. When the repairment is completed, the store will create a shipment and return the item to the customer.

- **Tracking Number not working Correctly**

The tracking number might delay inactivation. It can happen when a product misses its initial scanning at the shipping center. A tracking number will be activated the next time the product as an in-transit scanning occurring at many stages when in transit.

- **Shipment Stuck at Customs**

There are many reasons as to why a shipment might be delayed at the customs. The reasons can vary from high to low. The highest reason can be your products can be prohibited or low when you have the wrong paperwork. You can try the following to solve the issue:

- ✓ Directly contact your courier. Some premium courier also offers their services as brokers. So, they can be the people to help you out with this problem.

- ✓ There might be some outstanding taxes. Arrange to pay the taxes, so as the products can be released.

- ✓ Make sure there is no missing paperwork. Provide the customs with any additional required information, corrections, or paperwork that the customs require to complete the processing.

We make a tremendous effort to keep fraudsters away from our business. But at times, there are incidents there you will encounter some fraudsters. You should know how to handle them. Here are some ways you can protect yourself from fraud when shipping an item:

- **Online Tracking Shipment**

Retain a shipping service that offers online tracking for their shipments to confirm if your item was delivered. Online tracking services prove the item was delivered as compared to standard shipping receipts which, only shows the item was shipped.

- **Order Shipping Insurance**

There are many risks when shipping an item. It is important to purchase shipping insurance, especially when shipping fragile items. Shipping insurance has two main purposes. Insures the item from damages or loss and to help in tracking the item. The customers can be able to track their orders on route, and the business can know when the item was delivered.

- **Delay shipment for Risky Orders**

Consider delaying shipment for orders that are new and expensive and in demand, especially when shipping internationally.

- **Use the same retained shipping carrier**

Do not accept to use a different shipping carrier which the customer has requested when you are delivering the products to the customer. Instead, use the shipping carrier you have retained in all your shipping. There is a risk of the package rerouted by the customer to other addresses after delivery.

Documents Needed for Dropshipping

Dropshipping is such an easy business to get into! Glad you are looking into it. There are some essential legal documents required before starting a dropshipping company. Here are some of the documents needed. For your convenience, I will write the sequence in which you have to get these documents:

- **Company Registration Certificate**

A Company Registration Certificate is a document that shows you have formed and registered your company. In short, it's your company's birth certificate. Company Registration certificate shows the name of the company; it's registration number, and the date it was formed. It also indicates the type of company you set up and the registered location/address of the company.

- **Name Approval for your Business**

Businesses must have their names approved for their use before they proceed to registration. Sending an application for name approval can be denied for various reasons. If you are using an incorporation number as your business name, then name approval will not be required. Research your preferred name choices and make sure no one else is using the same name before you submit your request.

Save time by researching your preferred name choices before you apply. You can use the internet to search for available business and company names or hire the services of a qualified service provider to do this for you.

- **Company Bank Account Number**

When opening a Business Bank Account, your company registration certificate is one of the crucial documents you will need to take with you. It shows your business is set up correctly. Banks comply with rules and regulations to avoid risks like money laundering. They have to carry several checks before opening a new business account. It is why you need identification when opening an account.

- **A Sales Tax ID**

Most businesses are required to apply for a sales tax number. Unfortunately, most businesses don't know the reasons as to why their business needs a sales tax number to be allowed to operate and how they can apply for a sales tax number. Have you wondered what a sales tax number is? Here is a simple explanation to be able to understand what it is:

A sales tax number can also be called a Federal tax identification number. The sales tax number is used by the IRS to recognize your business for tax purposes. It can also be used by the IRS to track your business tax requirements. After you apply for a sales tax number, you will be given a Tax ID for your business. A Tax ID is used for quarterly and annual tax documents, and you will include it on any tax payments you make to the IRS.

- **Company Address Proof**

Company Address proof is a document confirming the location the business is, the name of the company, and the director of the company. It must have both your names and your address printed on it. The documents that are accepted as the address of proof are utility bills like water, gas, and electricity bills.

Chapter 9: The Technical Terms used in Dropshipping (Glossary)

Where you are a new supplier or an existing one in the online business, you need to be familiar with all the technical words and terminologies. These words will help in understanding all the processes and procedures when it comes to your business venture. It may seem like a very hectic process, but with time, you will be able to understand. Dropshipping seems to be a rather new concept in the online business. That is also another reason why you will need to understand the terms used, the products, terminologies, services, and the concept to easily manage your business in the drop-shipping field.

- **Dropshipping**: Traditionally, the retailers used to maintain their stock and inventory and then deliver to their customers. As for drop shipping, retailers do not manage the inventory. They will pass over their orders to a manufacturer, wholesaler, or a supplier. They will then do the order fulfillment to the customer. They are in charge of packaging and shipment.

- **E-commerce:** This involves buying and selling of your products on an electronic platform. This can be from a mobile application or over the internet. This mostly relates to online business and retailing.

- **Affiliate**: These are the owners of a site. Or the publishers who will likely recommend a retailer to introduce their customers to their goods. They will help retailers to generate more sales, leads, and traffic. The affiliate will then ask for a percentage of the sales revenue.

- **Affiliate Link**: These are URLs that have a number that qualifies the affiliate's performance. Affiliates are given the links by the retailers, and they can use that to advertise on their social media platforms, blogs, and content marketing. The identification number is normally attached to a specific URL. It is easier to track the number of traffic being generated by the link.

- **Blog:** These are websites that have short and updated articles about the products. They are commonly known as blog posts. They are also known as the digital journals highlighting products for sale. They are also a form of online marketing. You'll find retailers seeking the services of bloggers in order to promote their items. They will use what will call content marketing.

- **Distributor:** They act as a link between the manufacturer and the retailers. They will manage the products from the manufacturers and then sell that to the retailers. Distributors will always have a shorter time for shipping orders as compared to the manufacturers.

- **Inventory:** These are the good that a retailer has in stock. This will be in terms of the value or quantity. The level of stock at hand does not include what is to be delivered by the supplier. The accurate stock at hand is what is physically in the store. And what can be shipped out when ordered.

- **Manufacturer:** There are companies that are entitled to the production of goods and then sell them to different parties.

- **Gross Profit:** This is simply the gains achieved from the sales less the cost of production. It is simply computed as the revenue minus the expenses. For instance, when you have a sales revenue of $100, and the cost of goods sold is $20. Then your gross profit will be $80.

- **Net Profit:** Net profit is the sales revenue less all the expenses. It will include not only the cost of goods sold but also all the other expenses. Like marketing, salaries, operating, and miscellaneous expenses. It is the amount that if left when you've paid all the operating expenses.

- **Outsourcing:** Outsourcing is when a company will get the services of a third party. They will hire them in order to get a task executed and delivered. This is normally done for services that the company does not deliver.

- **Reseller:** These are businesses that will buy products for the purpose of selling them. And they will sell them at a profit and not for consumption purposes. Affiliates are also involved in becoming resellers as long they have their branded products.

- **Retailer:** These are companies that sell to the customers directly.

- **Supplier:** They are companies that will sell products to retailers, who will, in return, sell to their customers. They deal with either product, services or anything else that a consumer need.

- **Tracking Number:** These are the numbers that are used by shipping companies to track goods. They are alphanumeric form. They are normally used by companies like FedEx, USPS, and USPS. The reason for obtaining a tracking number is to ensure that both the sender and the receiver have information about the goods. They will know the product status, how it was shipped, and when it will be delivered.

- **Wholesaler:** These are companies that sell their products to their retailers. When a retailer makes a bulk order, they are always offered some discounts.

- **Authorization:** These are steps that are followed for payment processing. This is normally done when an order is submitted. The authorization must be done in order for the payment to be done. Authorization helps to know if there are enough funds in the account for the order to be completed.

- **Authorized Distributor:** These are companies that have been vetted and approved by the manufacturer to sell on their behalf. There are given the products to sell to retailers.

- **Authorized Retailer:** These are retailers that are allowed to sell products directly to customers on behalf of the manufacturer.

- **Chargeback:** This occurs when there is a refund. The refund is issued to the customer from the retailer. It will normally happen when there is a complaint. There are several reasons that can lead to that, poor quality, wrong delivery, or false advertising. When there are more chargebacks, this means that the retailer will pay more when processing payments.

- **Fulfillment:** This is the process whereby the product is assembled and prepared for shipment. This can also mean a third-party company will send its own products to customers on behalf of the retailer.

- **Listing Fees:** When a merchant lists their products on a third-party marketplace, there are costs associated with that. This is referred to as the listing fees. For instance, when you list on eBay, they will charge you for that.

- **Logistics:** This is a cycle that involves product management from their origin to when they are delivered in the e-commerce business, where drop shipping lies. Logistics is in terms of phases, from manufacturer to the customers. From transportation to delivery. From the manufacturer to the supplier, then to the retailer, and lastly to the final consumer.

- **Margin:** This is the difference between what is aid by the retailer and when the final customer will pay for the same product. That is what is known as profit. If the selling price is higher than the buying price, then that is a profit. If it is less, that will be a loss. For the retailer to have a higher margin, they can negotiate a lower price rate from the suppliers or increase their selling price.

- **Overhead:** These are all the products that relate to operating your business. It will not include direct expenses or materials. They include expenses like marketing cost, interest on loans, rent, maintenance, insurance, repairs, and legal fees.

- **Preferred Supplier:** These are suppliers that a retailer will prefer compared to the others. They are considered reliable and efficient, and they will be comfortable sourcing from them. They offer special prices and discounted rates. This will, in return, be beneficial to the supplier, less buying cost leads to higher selling prices. This leads to higher profits. They are advantageous to the retailer.

- **Address Verification System:** This is a system that is used to fight fraud associated with any payment. The system makes a comparison of the billing address that is used during checkout and the address on the card. When it does not match, it will indicate a purchase that considered fraudulent, and the payment will be declined. This will greatly help retailers in terms of reducing chargebacks.

- **Alibaba:** This is considered as one of the directories for dropshipping. It is an online marketplace that was established in China and is used worldwide. The website millions of customers; from retailers to customers. Over the years, it has recorded more sales than any other e-commerce in the world.

- **AliExpress:** This is a marketplace with an online presence and with an international touch. It is owned by Alibaba too. It is mostly used by smaller retailers and businesses; they can list their products and sell them in the global village.

- **Amazon:** This is another dropshipping directory that is also considered an online marketplace. It is considered the largest online marketplace in the world. With the highest revenue generation and market capitalization. Most of the people who benefit from this platform and third-party retailers. They are known to bring over half of revenue for Amazon.

- **eBay:** This is another dropshipping directory; it is an online marketplace that deals with one consumer to another and one business party to a consumer. eBay was traditionally known for auctions that were done online. It allows retailers to list their products and increase their market base. It is popularly considered by huge companies and smaller business ventures.

- **Manufacturer Suggested Retail Price:** This is what is commonly known as MSRP. It is the price that a manufacturer will recommend as the selling price for its products to the consumers. A retailer has the liberty to sell at the suggested MSRP or at their own price that can be higher in order to give higher margins.

- **Minimum Advertised Price:** This is popularly known as MAP. This is the minimum price allowed to advertise a product. It cannot go any lesser than the MAP. When you decide to sell from the manufacturer, you will have to adhere to their rule on the MAP.

- **PayPal:** This is an online payment method. It offers a platform to do online purchases and transfers. And the good news is that it supports several online purchases and platforms.

- **Bootstrapping:** This falls under the mode of capital to start your dropshipping business. This is a self-funding method for a new business venture. Their operating expenses are paid from their profits or investments. They do not have external sources of funds.

- **Capture:** After authorization is done, there is a need to secure your payments. The process is what is known as capture.

- **Confirmed Shipping Address:** This is the address that is based on information issued of the package to be delivered. Or the address the customer has registered for their payment.

- **Conversion:** This is when an individual completes their marketing plans or goals. It is commonly referred to as when an individual will change to a customer and will make a sale.

- **Customer Relationship Management:** This is also known as CRM; this is a software that is used for organizing and automating information and relationship in the business.

- **Directories:** There are sites that will list other companies and link them to the sites. Most of the online stores are referred to as directories.

- **Domain:** This is the address of a website where you can do your listing or view products.

- **Expedited Shipping:** It is a shipping option that involves having handling charges that are reduced. Customers will pay a premium cost to make sure that what they ordered is delivered fast.

- **Exporting:** This involves selling products to retailers or wholesalers who are in another country.

- **Fraud:** It is the deception that is done intentionally in order to gain something illegally.

- **Fulfillment:** This is the process whereby order is fulfilled or completed. A third-party can also use this term and ship products on behalf of the manufacturer.

- **Minimum Order Quantity:** Also known as MOQ, most manufacturers will need the retailers to buy products on minimum order. When that is not met, the order is not processed.

- **Niche:** This is the market segment.

- **Search Engine Optimization:** This is the process whereby the search on the website is made easier. It is popularly known as SEO.

- **Per Order Fee:** It occurs when a manufacturer drops ships the customer's order. When it is done directly on behalf of the retailer, the manufacturer will then charge his fees as per order.

- **Shipping:** This is the movement of products from one point to another from the origin like the manufacturer to the customer's destination.

Conclusion

Thank you for making it through to the end of *Dropshipping E-Commerce: A Must-read Beginner's Guide to Dropshipping on How to Customize Your Own Brand Store, Find the Best Niche Content Which Will Keep Customers Coming Back!*

We hope that you found the book to be informative and educative. This should be your guide in the dropshipping business. It will help you start your business and manage it. This interactive book has enabled you to know about dropshipping and its pros and cons. The practical examples that will in sharpening your skills and become a successful businessperson.

By now, you know about the ordering process, how to spot any good suppliers, and how to eliminate the bad ones. In dropshipping, the supply chain is very important. And by now, you know how the supply chain moves and its benefits. The Oberlo is an essential app, and we believe you've learned more about it. You know how to spot the features, the advantages, and the disadvantages.

Another very important aspect of dropshipping is the supplier's directory. We hope you have appreciated the concept of the directory, and it is one aspect that will make you successful in this business.

When pricing your products, it is good to know about the pricing strategy. This helps in having the right price and the correct margin. With the glossary outlined, this is a sure way to ensure that you understand everything about dropshipping.

We thank you again for choosing to download this book. We believe you did find the book educative and engaging. A positive review and comment on Amazon will be appreciated.

form the information ultimately takes. This includes copied versions of the work both physical, digital and audio unless express consent of the Publisher is provided beforehand. Any additional rights reserved.

Furthermore, the information that can be found within the pages described forthwith shall be considered both accurate and truthful when it comes to the recounting of facts. As such, any use, correct or incorrect, of the provided information will render the Publisher free of responsibility as to the actions taken outside of their direct purview. Regardless, there are zero scenarios where the original author or the Publisher can be deemed liable in any fashion for any damages or hardships that may result from any of the information discussed herein.

Additionally, the information in the following pages is intended only for informational purposes and should thus be thought of as universal. As befitting its nature, it is presented without assurance regarding its prolonged validity or interim quality. Trademarks that are mentioned are done without written consent and can in no way be considered an endorsement from the trademark holder.